# PEGGY MARTIN

# PAPER PIECE
## the Quick-Strip Way

Complete Projects • Create Your Own Designs • Paper Piece Faster!

C&T PUBLISHING

Text © 2007 Phyllis Golloway Martin

Artwork © 2007 C&T Publishing, Inc.

Publisher: Amy Marson

Editorial Director: Gailen Runge

Acquisitions Editor: Jan Grigsby

Editor: Deb Rowden

Technical Editors: Carolyn Aune, Deborah Dubois

Copyeditor/Proofreader: Wordfirm Inc.

Cover Designer: Kristen Yenche

Design Director/Book Designer: Kristen Yenche

Illustrator: Wendy Mathson

Production Coordinators: Zinnia Heinzmann, Kerry Graham

Photography: Luke Mulks unless otherwise noted

Published by C&T Publishing, Inc., P.O. Box 1456, Lafayette, CA 94549

Front cover: *Starlight, Starbright* by Patricia Wolfe

Back cover: *Cactus Tree* (detail, top) and *Star Dance*, both by the author

Library of Congress Cataloging-in-Publication Data

Martin, Peggy.
  Paper piece the quick-strip way : 12 complete projects--create your own designs--paper piece faster / Peggy Martin.
      p. cm.
  ISBN-13: 978-1-57120-368-7 (paper trade : alk. paper)
  ISBN-10: 1-57120-368-0 (paper trade : alk. paper)
 1. Patchwork--Patterns. 2. Patchwork quilts. 3. Strip quilting. I. Title.

  TT835.M2736126 2007
  746.46'041--dc22
                                    2006016987

Printed in China

10 9 8 7 6 5 4 3 2 1

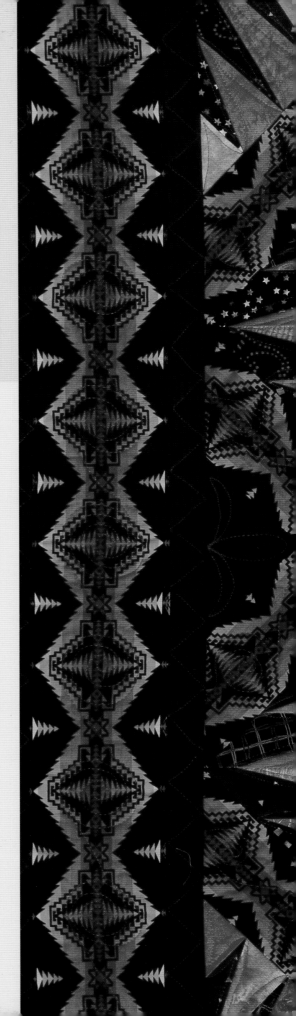

# CONTENTS

# DEDICATION

To quilters everywhere who find comfort in the warmth of colors and fabrics and whose generosity and creativity continue to amaze and inspire me—may you have the courage to travel your own path, express yourself in cloth, and have great fun in the process!

# ACKNOWLEDGMENTS

Thanks to all the quilters; it would have been impossible to create a book without your dedication and hard work. Your wonderful talents are greatly appreciated! Thank you to Mary Lou Betts, Kris Blundell-Mitchell, Lisa Coulombe, Annette Friedlein, Shelley Gragg, Michelle Hamand, Joan Hamilton, Linda Kamm, Lorraine Marstall, Wendy Mathson, Sandra McCullough, Jean Nagy, Lee Olson, Yvonne Regala, Karen Shell, Mary Tabar, and Pat Wolfe.

A big note of thanks to my editors, Deb Rowden, Carolyn Aune, and Diane Pederson—your guidance and talents helped me immeasurably. Jan Grigsby, Mari Dreyer, and all the rest of the great C&T staff have been such a great help in many ways over the years—thank you all!

Special thanks to Wendy Mathson, the computer graphics genius who helped make everything accurate and bailed me out more than once when time was tight. Thanks to Linda Kamm for her incredible longarm artistry in quilting many of the quilts for this book. Thank you to Nancy Amidon and Amidon Quiltworks for providing workshop space.

And a very special thanks to my family: my husband, David, whose support has enabled me to teach quilting and travel over the years; my son Michael, whose computer expertise and patience in helping me learn have been immensely helpful; and my son Ryan, who always keeps me on my toes and helps me see my quilts and the world through different eyes.

# INTRODUCTION

Over the years, it has been my mission to make quilting faster, easier, and more fun. Up until now, I have mainly concentrated on sewing techniques. With this book, I can't wait to share with you how fun and easy it can be to design your own blocks and quilts as well! Many quilters fear the design process, thinking that they need an art background or a great deal of experience. The word *drafting* terrifies them, making them think they must have a great deal of knowledge in math or geometry.

With the new, easy methods I have developed, designing blocks for paper piecing is as easy as drawing a line. (And no, you don't even have to be able to draw a straight line—that's what rulers are for!)

After the release of my first book, *Quick-Strip Paper Piecing*, quilters were requesting more patterns that could be paper pieced in this revolutionary new way. In this book, I am including more patterns and projects, but I am also showing you how easy it is to design your **own** blocks. Because these blocks are made up of repeat units, just a few lines drawn in each unit can produce quite stunning results. In addition to learning how to design your own blocks, you'll discover how much fun it is to use blocks in different ways to affect the overall design of the quilt. Some of the design principles I have experimented with are positive/negative colorations, changing backgrounds in the quilt, and using portions of blocks as borders or setting triangles. The results of these experiments are often surprising and always rewarding.

Easy design exercises and examples are included in the design section. For those of you who are new to Quick-Strip Paper Piecing, full instructions are given for sewing with this fast and easy method in the technique section. Patterns and instructions are provided for twelve projects, with different design possibilities to give you even more ideas. I hope these ideas will spark your imagination to produce quilts that truly reflect your own personal design sense.

# FROM BLOCK DESIGN
## TO QUILT DESIGN

Quick-Strip Paper Piecing is a faster, easier way to paper piece using repeat units to make stars, pinwheels, flowers, and other designs. It is amazingly easy to design your own blocks for this method. Beginning with a simple shape and just adding a few lines, you'll be producing your own designs in no time! Design units for various types of blocks are included at the end of this chapter. After you design your block, the designing of the quilt itself is the next step. Let's go through a few simple exercises to show you how easy designing can be.

## Drafting supplies for block design

Mechanical pencil and eraser

A black permanent fine-line pen

A see-through drafting ruler with a ⅛″ grid (12″ or 18″ size is good)

Tracing paper

A compass

## Dividing a block for design

With this design method, the block is divided into smaller units, which will be repeated to make the design. There are many ways a quilt block can be broken up into smaller units. Here are some of my favorite divisions:

*Squares*

*Half-square triangles*

*Octagon triangles*

*Octagon kites*

*Hexagon triangles*

*Hexagon kites*

*Circle segments*

## Design basics

I like to begin designing on a smaller scale to try out designs before drafting a full-size pattern. The process is fairly simple. Select the block division you would like to use. Trace the small design unit, then add various design lines. Trace your design into a small block to see what it will look like before it is drafted full size. Pages 22–28 contain small design units and full-size units for creating your own designs for 12″ blocks. The small design units are one-fourth the size of the full-size units—another way to look at it is that everything you draw on the small unit will be four times larger on the full-size pattern. I have chosen the octagon kite unit to demonstrate the various steps in the design process.

**1.** Using the design units on page 25, trace an octagon kite design unit on tracing paper with a drafting ruler and a pencil. The center blue line is just a guideline for drafting accurately centered points, so just trace it very lightly. On another sheet of tracing paper, trace the design block. On the octagon kite unit, lay the ruler across the kite shape, from upper left to lower right, and draw a diagonal line from one side of the unit to the other. On the design block sheet, trace the diagonal line from the kite unit into the 8 kite units in the square, rotating the square around as you trace, to see the resulting block. Just 1 diagonal line on the octagon kite unit, repeated 8 times in the square, will produce a simple star:

*One diagonal line added*

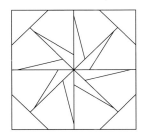

*Design unit repeated to form a star*

**2.** Add another diagonal line to make a star point on the other side. To make the star symmetrical, you will need to place the ruler the same distance from the top point of the unit and the same distance from the bottom edge. First, using the ruler or a compass, measure the distance along the left side from the top point to the beginning of the line you drew. Measure the same distance on the right side from the top point and put a little mark with your pencil. Measure the distance to the bottom point on the right, and then place a mark on the left side at the same measurement. Lay the ruler across the 2 new points (from upper right to lower left) and draw the new line, stopping the line when it meets the first line you drew. When the units are traced onto the design square, the points will meet and have the same thickness because they have been drawn symmetrically.

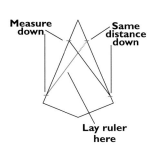

*Measuring down on each side*
*Drawing the second design line*

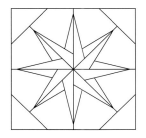

*Symmetrical star design*

*Dimensional Stars* is a quilt I made using this simple star. I alternated backgrounds between black and white on every other star. The corner triangles were also alternated between black and white to produce another design around each star.

*Dimensional Stars*, by Peggy Martin, 2005. Quilt size: 47″ × 47″.

If the points are placed differently on the second line, the points will not meet when the design is traced, and an asymmetrical star will be formed. I like to make the difference very noticeable, so it looks deliberate. If there is only a very slight difference, it just looks like you didn't piece it right!

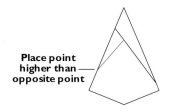

*Asymmetrical unit*

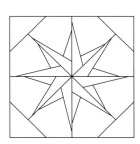

*Asymmetrical star*

**3.** Now let's add a third point. For a symmetrical point, using the symmetrical design you drew in Step 2 above, use your ruler or compass to measure the same distance from the top corner on each side and make a mark for each measurement. Place the ruler from the mark on each side across the unit, and draw the lines to form another point, stopping a line when it meets a previously drawn line. If you have drawn the point symmetrically, it should fall on the light blue center guideline. Trace the units to see the resulting star.

 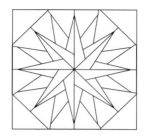

*Drawing lines for another point*     *Star with symmetrical points added*

Again, you have the option of making this point asymmetrical, simply by placing the ruler wherever you wish to form the next star point, ignoring the center guideline.

You could add this point either to a symmetrical or asymmetrical star, depending on the look you want.

 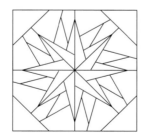

*Adding asymmetrical point to symmetrical unit*     *Symmetrical star with asymmetrical point added*

A different strategy for producing a design is to use lines that echo each other, as in the Star Dance block on page 42. Notice the small block design on the pattern page. This block is a very easy one to design and sew because there are no points to match.

Create patterns with other lines, points, radiating lines, zigzags, or other ideas you would like to try out to produce your own designs. Try to avoid having a lot of lines come together at one point; this produces a lot of bulk and is hard to sew. Keep in mind that you will want to be able to piece these designs, so remember that the seams in the design must be able to be sewn in a particular order.

## NUMBERING THE ORDER OF SEWING

Look at the design and figure out the order in which the seams will be sewn. Many designs have several possibilities, so use a pencil and try the numbers in various sequences. Determine where you will need to begin. Generally speaking, where you stopped designing is where you will begin sewing; the smallest line you drew is **usually** where you will need to begin with number 1 (it is kind of a backward process). Remember that it is possible to design something that cannot be sewn without breaking the pattern up into smaller pieces (see page 10). If your pattern needs modifying to make it possible to sew the design more easily, now is the time to redraft the difficult or impossible areas. When you are satisfied that the block can be sewn, number each area in order.

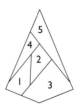

*Numbering a design*

## DESIGN PROBLEMS AND SOLUTIONS

It is possible to design things that are impossible to paper piece; however, sometimes the block can be broken down into several different segments to make more complex designs workable.

Below are two examples of unsewable design problems with their solutions.

In the original design below, the pattern as drafted cannot be sewn. When area 4 is sewn and flipped back, the seam line where 4 touches 2 will be a raw edge. To fix this problem, there are two solutions. Solution 1 is to split the pattern into two units, piece each separately, then seam the two units together. Solution 2 is to simply redraw the seam lines for area 3 and area 4 as shown below. The pattern can be easily sewn when the seam lines are rearranged in this manner, making solution 2 the better option for this particular design problem.

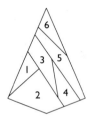 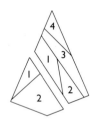 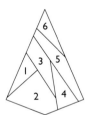

*Original design* *Solution 1* *Solution 2*
*cannot be sewn*

The original design below also cannot be sewn as drafted. When area 6 is pieced, the seam line where 6 touches 4 will be a raw edge. The easiest solution to this problem is to split the design down the middle and piece it as two separate units, A and B, which will then be seamed together. This solution does change the appearance of the center star slightly, but it is the easiest solution to the design problem.

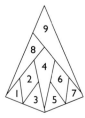 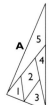

*Original design* *Solution*
*cannot be sewn*

## Designing with other units

As previously mentioned, a block can be divided in many different ways. The same basic steps are used to design with other block division units.

### DESIGNING WITH SQUARES

The design templates for square design units are on page 22. The full-size pattern unit is 6″ square, with 4 patterns used to make a 12″ block. Designs can be repeated in the same orientation from square to square, like tiles, or they can be turned or rotated around the center to make stars or a variety of designs.

Michelle Hamand's quilt *Navigation* was designed to represent the star logo of Nichols Elementary School in Oceanside, California, where she teaches first grade. She was easily able to translate the school's star logo into a pattern using square units, which were then rotated to make the star.

*Navigation*, by Michelle Hamand, 2005. Quilt size: 24″ x 24″.

*Navigation design unit*

## DESIGNING WITH HALF-SQUARE TRIANGLES

The design templates for half-square triangle units are on page 23. When designing with half-square triangles, the most common strategy is to design in one of the triangles and then mirror image that design in the adjacent triangle. First choose one of the triangles and draft a design. On another piece of paper, trace the block design unit, and then trace the triangle you designed in all four of those triangles on the block design unit. Turn the tracing paper over and trace the original triangle design on the **back side** of the tracing paper in the remaining four triangles to produce the mirror image.

Pat Wolfe's quilt *Fractured Rainbow* showcases her original block, designed using half-square triangles. Her mirror-image design produces a marvelous network of bright colors that appear to fracture and float on the black background.

Mirror imaging is the most common design technique to use with half-square triangles, but there are other design ideas that work equally well. In my quilt *Stellar Jewels*, I did one corner of the design as a repeat (not mirror imaged) and the other corners where the blocks come together as a mirror image.

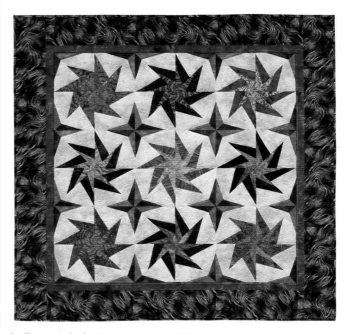

*Stellar Jewels*, by Peggy Martin, 2005. Quilt size: 48″ × 48″.

Stellar Jewels *design unit*

*Fractured Rainbow*, by Patricia Wolfe, 2005. Quilt size: 26″ × 26″.

Fractured Rainbow *design unit*

## DESIGNING WITH HEXAGONS

The design templates for hexagon divisions are on pages 26 and 27. Just like the octagon, the hexagon can be divided into either a triangle shape or a kite shape. Each of these units has a blue centerline for drafting reference. Six units repeat to make the design. Hexagons can nest together on the quilt surface, like traditional Grandmother's Flower Garden blocks, or triangles can be sewn in the corners to square off the hexagon. After the triangles are added, the block will be a rectangle instead of a square. Strips can be added to make the block into a 12″ square. Look at the snowflake quilts on pages 79 and 86 to see blocks made using the hexagon kite unit.

Mary Tabar designed *Shifting Reflections* by enlarging a hexagon unit, splitting it in half on the center blue line, then dividing it into several different sections. A design was drafted in each section. Those designs were then mirror imaged in the other half of the hexagon unit. This mirror imaging of the designs produces a kaleidoscopic effect. The border completes the central design, with lines that appear to cross under the inner dark border.

*Shifting Reflections*, by Mary Tabar, 2005. Quilt size: 54″ x 54″.

## DESIGNING WITH CIRCLES

A circle can be divided into any number of subdivisions, but dividing it into eight units is an easy way to start, and one of my favorite ways to work. Design templates for circle units are on page 28. Designing with this circle unit is just like designing with octagon divisions, and the unit will be similar in appearance except that the outer edges will be rounded instead of straight. The Evening Star block (page 96) was designed using a circle with eight subdivisions.

Wendy Mathson's and Lisa Coulombe's quilt, *Palm Star Aglow*, was inspired by the traditional Palm Leaf block (see page 54). The design was expanded and drafted into an enlarged circle wedge. A variety of rich batik fabrics form the color palette.

*Palm Star Aglow*, by Wendy Mathson and Lisa Coulombe, 2005. Quilt size: 56½″ x 56½″.

# Making the full-size pattern

## REVERSING THE DESIGN

Because the fabric is placed on the back side of the paper pattern in paper piecing, the finished block will be a **mirror image** of the pattern. If you want your finished block to look **exactly** like the block you drafted, turn the traced design **over** before you make the actual full-size pattern, so you will see the mirror image as you draft the final design.

## NUMBERING THE AREAS

Transfer the numbers from your original design to each area, remembering to place them in the correct sequence and position if you have made your pattern as a mirror image.

## FROM DESIGN UNIT TO FULL-SIZE PATTERN

The patterns for the full-size units for each shape are located on the same page as the small design units. Notice that the seam allowance has been added to the full-size unit. **Do all measuring and designing on the inner sewing lines of the unit, *not* on the outer dashed seam-allowance line.** This keeps the pattern true to the original design.

> **tip** When drafting your final pattern, consider drawing the outer star points slightly in from the bottom edge of the full-size unit. This will help prevent points from being cut off when the block is sewn together.

There are two basic methods for enlarging the design unit into the full-size pattern.

Method 1. **Enlarging by hand.** Copy or trace the full-size design unit for the shape you need. If you need the center blue line as a reference point, trace it in very lightly; it will not be part of the final pattern. The full-size units are four times larger than the small design units. To exactly reproduce the small unit in the full-size pattern, measure the distances for ruler placement on the small unit you made and multiply the measurements by four to translate them onto the full-size pattern. Rather than measuring precisely, sometimes I just look at the small design and try to approximate the same look on the full-size pattern. Use the same drafting techniques that you used on the small design to draft the full-size pattern. When designing symmetrical blocks, I find that measuring the distances with a compass to mark each side is often easier and more accurate than using a ruler. Try to draft the patterns as accurately as possible so any points that need to match will be accurate.

Method 2. **Enlarging with a copy machine.** Enlarge the small design unit 400% (or, if your copier does not go to 400%, enlarge the copy 200%, then enlarge that copy 200%) and you will get a design four times larger. The enlarged design will have lines that are too thick to be precise for a pattern, and they may not be exactly accurate. Using tracing paper, place a traced copy of the full-size unit over the enlarged photocopy and trace the design lines, correcting any distortion that the copy machine might have created.

## FINALIZING THE PATTERN

Extend any lines that go to the outside edge all the way across the seam allowance to the outer edge of the pattern. This makes sewing easier. When the drafted design is completed, draw in the lines with a permanent fine-point pen. This will help the pattern reproduce more clearly when you are making copies. Write the numbers for the sewing order in each area.

## MEASURING THE PATTERN FOR STRIP SIZES

Measure each area of the pattern, beginning with area 1. Lay the ¼" line of a wide ruler (I use my 6" rotary cutting ruler) on the sewing line between area 1 and area 2. Look down to the widest place on area 1 and check that measurement on the ruler, rounding up to the nearest ¼". Add ½" to that measurement for the seam allowance. You have added a total of ¾" for the seam allowance, rather than the exact ½" amount. This extra amount in the seam allowance gives you a little leeway, which is helpful in paper piecing. Mark this total measurement in the design area of the pattern using a permanent pen.

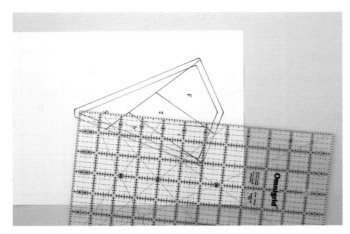

*Measuring for strip sizes*

## ADDING ARROWS

To add arrows for the Quick-Strip Paper Piecing method, position the pattern so that number 1 is on the **left** and number 2 is on the **right**. Draw arrows pointing **away** from you in area 1 and area 2. Move your pattern so number 3 is to the **right** of the lower numbers, and draw the arrow **away** from you. Continue adding arrows to each piecing area in the same manner, rotating the pattern as necessary to keep the higher numbered space to your right. See page 32 for a more detailed explanation of how to use the arrows when sewing.

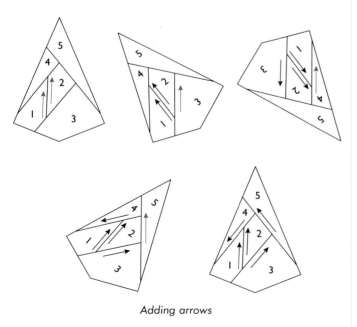

*Adding arrows*

## MAKING COPIES OF THE PATTERN

For 12″ blocks, make four copies of the square pattern, four **each** of the half-square triangles, six of hexagon patterns, and eight of octagon patterns and circle patterns. Cut them out and you are ready to sew using the Quick-Strip Paper Piecing method described on pages 29–39.

## SEWING A TEST BLOCK AND FIGURING YARDAGE

I always sew a test block of any pattern I design, before beginning on a quilt. That way I make sure the pattern sews easily and all the measurements have been made accurately. Sometimes a design may need a little adjusting to make it more sewable, so testing the pattern first can save a lot of frustration!

To figure yardage, keep track of how many strips you need to cut to sew each area. Multiply the number of strips needed for one block by the number of blocks you want to make for your quilt, and that will tell you how many strips to cut for the whole quilt. To figure yardage, multiply the number of strips needed by the width of each strip. This gives you the total inches of fabric needed. Divide that number by 36 to get the amount needed in yards.

> Number of strips × width of 1 strip = inches of fabric needed ÷ 36 = total yardage for each area

Remember to add some extra (maybe an extra ⅛ or ¼ yard) to the total measurement for that "fudge factor," in case any mistakes are made in cutting or sewing!

See how fun and easy it is to be your own designer? You can adapt these techniques to many other shapes, or subdivide existing shapes to make more complicated designs. Your imagination will take you as far as you want to go!

## Designing a quilt with your original blocks

Now that you have designed your own block, you can experiment with different design ideas for the quilt itself. Changing background colors in different areas of the quilt is one way to add design interest. In many of the quilts in this book, I have experimented with alternating two different background colors. *Dimensional Stars* (page 8), *Star Dance* (page 41), *Autumn Dance* (page 45), and *Dusk to Dawn* (page 70) are examples of quilts in which two different background colors have been alternated.

## BLOCKS THAT FORM SECONDARY PATTERNS

Designing a block that will make a secondary pattern when the blocks are sewn next to each other is a classic design strategy. *Stellar Jewels* (page 11) was designed to form a four-pointed star at the corners where the blocks come together.

*Bull's Eye* (below) has star designs in the center of each block, with patterns that resemble the spokes of a wheel forming where the blocks come together.

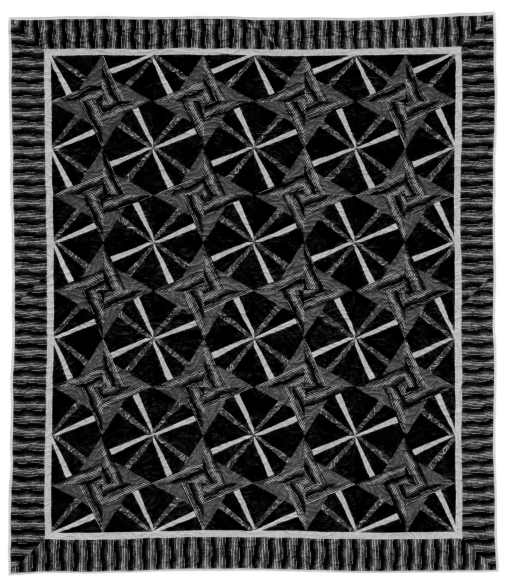

*Bull's Eye,* by Yvonne Regala, 2005. Quilt size: 57″ × 68″.

## SPLITTING BLOCKS

Sections of blocks can be used as design elements, giving the appearance that the block has been split. In the quilts *Star Dance* (page 41) and *Autumn Dance* (page 45), portions of Star Dance blocks are used as borders, producing a medallion effect. This block is based on the octagon kite unit, which works well for borders. In *Light Up the Fourth* (detail, right), Lorraine Marstall takes the Star Dance block a step further by mirror imaging a portion of the block to form the border design. The corner designs in the border are simplified versions of the pattern and its mirror image.

Detail of *Light Up the Fourth*, by Lorraine Marstall. Full quilt shown on page 52.

Half-square triangle block divisions can also easily be used as borders. Portions of the Wishing Star block are used as a border in *Tequila Star Rise* (page 62).

Joan Hamilton's *Summer Salsa* quilt (below) features her original circle block design with asymmetrical points. She colored the quilt in bright citrus colors and used segments of the blocks to surround the center circle.

*Summer Salsa,* by Joan M. Hamilton, 2005. Quilt size: 20½" × 30".

## BLOCKS SET ON POINT WITH PIECED TRIANGLE CORNERS

Many blocks completely change their appearance when they are set on point, and I often design a block with the idea that it will be set on point in the quilt. As much as I like the look of blocks on point, I don't always want to sew them as a diagonal set. By setting a square on point and adding corner triangles to it, the block once again becomes a square and can be sewn into the quilt in straight horizontal and vertical rows. This is the same design principle used with the traditional Diamond in the Square block.

*Diamond in the Square*

To add more design interest, the corner triangles can also be pieced. I was delighted when I realized that two half-square triangle block divisions from a 12″ block will automatically fit the corner triangles of any 12″ block set on point. Not only will they make a great design in the corners, but there are two design options for setting the triangles together.

With the Palm Leaf block (pattern on page 58), for example, the two triangles that form the block are sewn together on the diagonal seam to make the traditional square block:

*Palm Leaf block sewn on diagonal seam*

When the triangles are sewn together on the side seams instead, a triangle is formed that will measure 12″ on the long side and can be used as a corner triangle with any 12″ block set on point in the Diamond in the Square setting. Two different designs can be made by sewing the two different sides of the Palm Leaf triangles together:

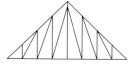

*Sawtooth Palm Leaf triangle*

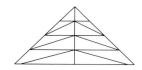

*Flying Geese Palm Leaf triangle*

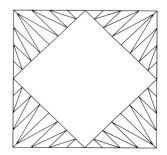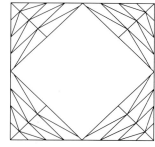

*Pieced triangles added to block corners*

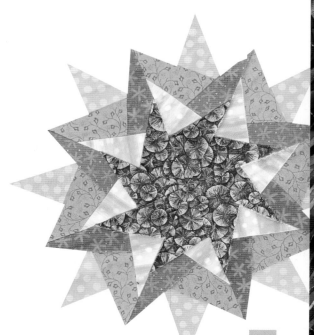

Mary Lou Betts used the Flying Geese Palm Leaf corner triangles with a star block she designed in her quilt *Desert Star* (below). The pieced corners add a wonderful frame to the central block.

*Dusk to Dawn* (page 70) also has Flying Geese Palm Leaf corner triangles, this time framing the Wishing Star block. Note the Palm Leaf blocks that form where the blocks come together.

These triangle units can also be used as borders. In *Night Fire* (page 74), the central Wishing Star block is framed with Sawtooth Palm Leaf corner triangles. More Sawtooth Palm Leaf units are used as borders to produce a medallion effect.

The Wishing Star block is also set on point and portions of the block are used as corner triangles in *Starlight, Starbright* on page 66 and *Starry Glow* on page 69. Notice that where four corner triangles come together, another Wishing Star block is formed in the center.

## COMBINING MULTIPLE BLOCKS FOR QUILT DESIGNS

Combining different blocks that complement each other is a great way to make a quilt with a lot of design interest. Karen Shell's *Discovery* began with an Evening Star block (pattern on page 96) in the center with half blocks on the top and bottom borders. Circles of her own design are "split" and used as side borders and corners.

*Desert Star*, by Mary Lou Betts, 2005. Quilt size: 23″ × 23″.

*Discovery*, by Karen Shell, 2005. Quilt size: 33″ × 33″. Machine quilted by Michaelanne Gephart.

*Road Through the Cosmos*, by Joan M. Hamilton, 2005.
Quilt size: 18″ × 22″.

Joan Hamilton designed several circular stars inspired by Mariner's Compass designs in her quilt *Road Through the Cosmos*. The stars diminish in size as they appear to travel away from the viewer on a curving paper-pieced pathway.

Kris Blundell-Mitchell adapted the Palm Leaf block to form elongated palm fronds swaying over a tropical appliquéd landscape in her quilt *Memories of Hawaii*. She added a tiny Wishing Star block in the lower right-hand corner, reminiscent of the mariner's compass used on old sea charts. Using a copy machine or scanner, any block can be changed to whatever size you wish to add just the right design element to your quilt.

*Memories of Hawaii*, by Kris Blundell-Mitchell, 2005.
Quilt size: 36″ × 30″.

*The Powers of Flowers*, by Linda Kamm, 2005.
Quilt size: 58½″ × 72″.

Palm Leaf blocks were the initial inspiration for *The Powers of Flowers*, by Linda Kamm. Linda designed a number of her own original flower and leaf blocks using square and half-square triangle units to elaborate on the garden theme. The blocks were then set in an innovative arrangement, giving the quilt a delightful contemporary flair.

*Timeless Mariner*, designed by Shelley Gragg, 2005. Quilt size: 91″ x 91″.
Pieced and appliquéd by members of Friendship Quilters of San Diego,
and machine quilted by Lois Russell. Photo by Sharon Risedorph.

Shelley Gragg drafted intricate Mariner's Compass blocks and alternated them
with appliqué blocks in a fleur-de-lis design. A border with Celtic appliqué
and Evening Star blocks in the corners completed her quilt design for *Timeless
Mariner*. This quilt is a wonderful example of how well appliqué and pieced
blocks work together. Blocks were made by various members of Friendship
Quilters of San Diego. This quilt was the group's opportunity quilt for 2006.

# Square units

Design units are one-fourth the size of a full-size unit.

*Square design unit*

*Square design block*

*Make 4 for a 12˝ block.*

# Half-square triangle units

Design units are one-fourth the size of a full-size unit.

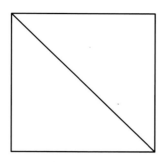

*Half-square triangle
design unit*

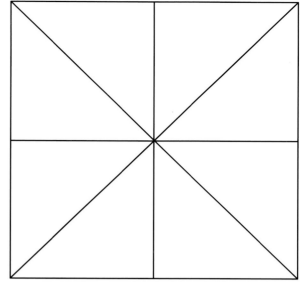

*Half-square triangle design block*

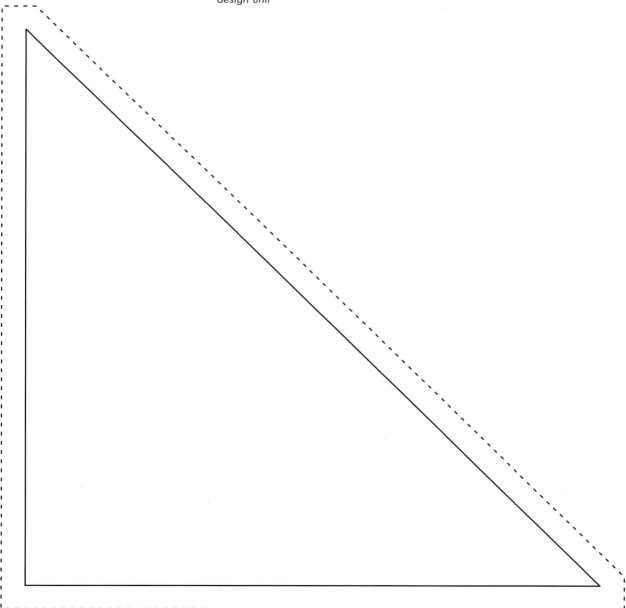

*Make 8 for a 12″ block.*

# Octagon triangle units

Design units are one-fourth the size of a full-size unit.

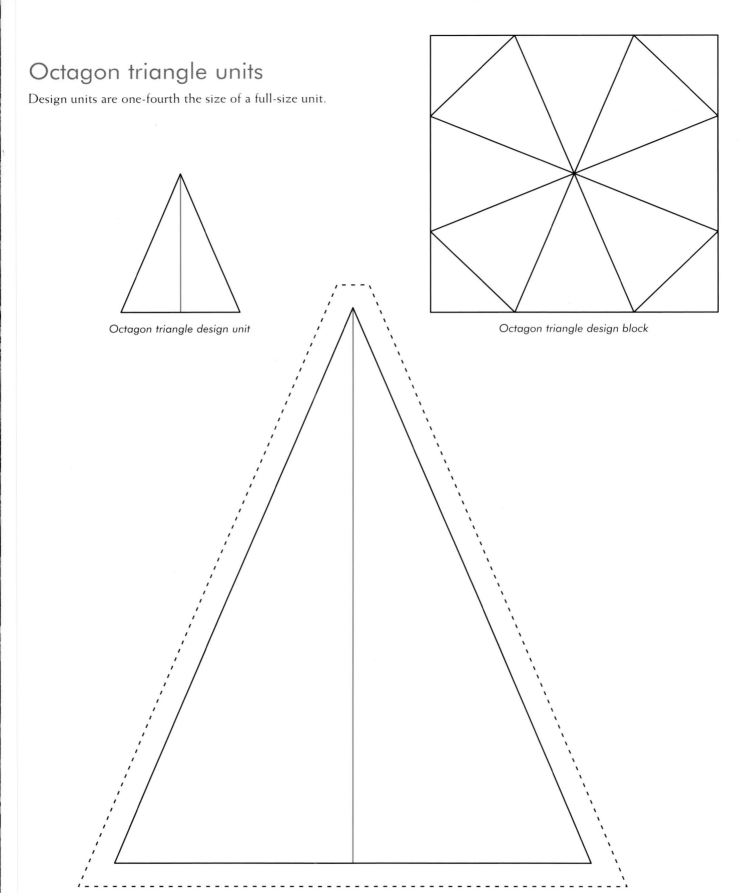

*Octagon triangle design unit*

*Octagon triangle design block*

*Make 8 for a 12" block. Cut two 4½" squares.*
*Cut each once on the diagonal for the 4 corner triangles.*

# Octagon kite units

Design units are one-fourth the size of a full-size unit.

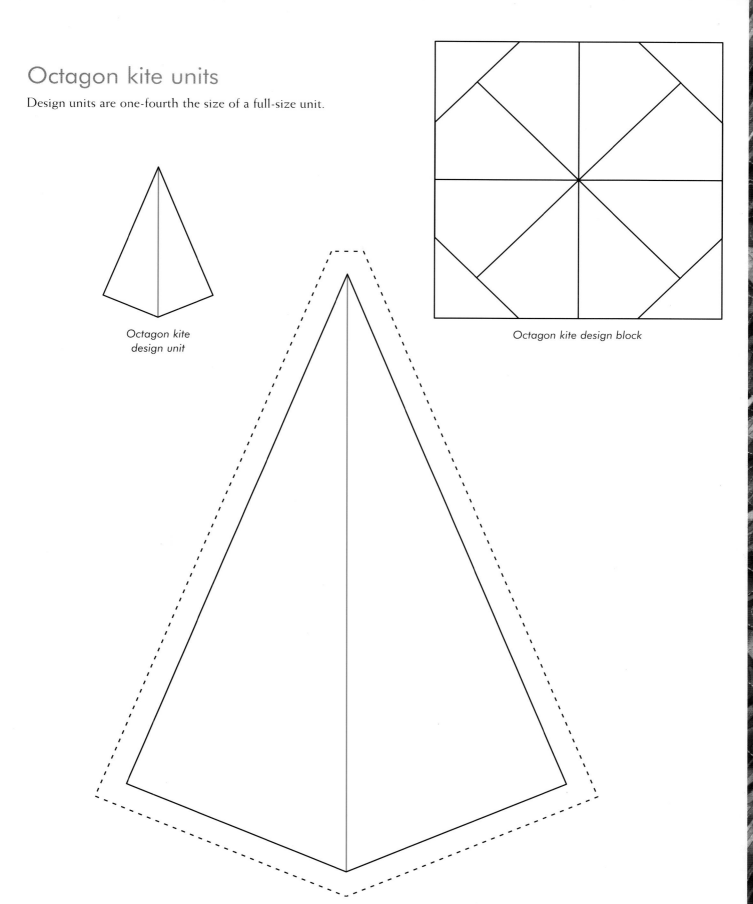

*Octagon kite
design unit*

*Octagon kite design block*

*Make 8 for a 12″ block. Cut two 4½″ squares.
Cut each once on the diagonal for the 4 corner triangles.*

# Hexagon triangle units

Design units are one-fourth the size of a full-size unit.

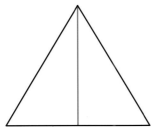

*Hexagon triangle design unit*

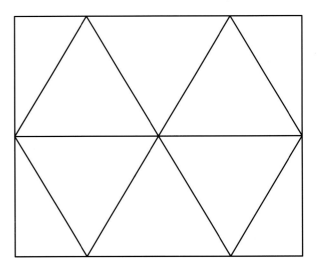

*Hexagon triangle design block*

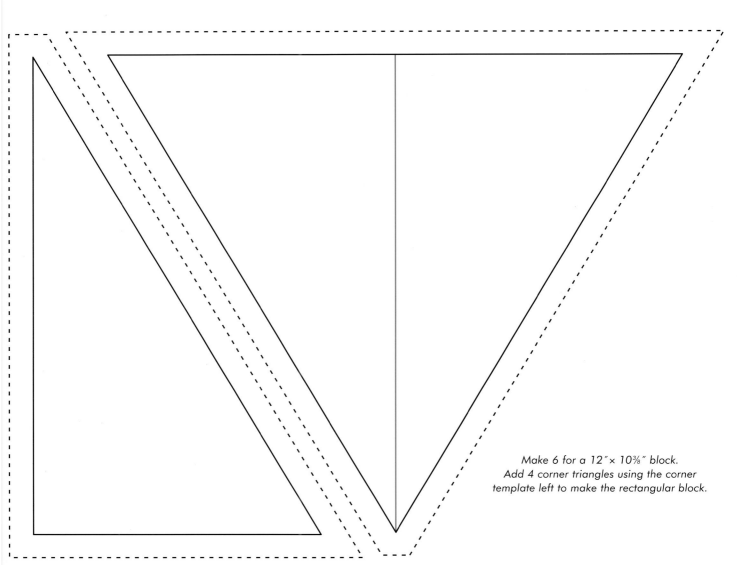

*Make 6 for a 12″ × 10⅜″ block.
Add 4 corner triangles using the corner
template left to make the rectangular block.*

*Corner template pattern for hexagon block; cut 2 and 2 reversed.*

# Hexagon kite units

Design units are one-fourth the size of a full-size unit.

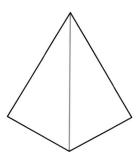

*Hexagon kite design unit*

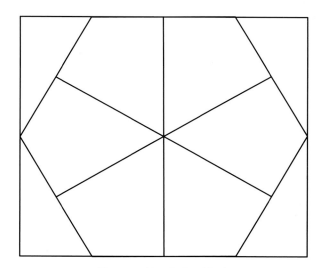

*Hexagon kite design block*

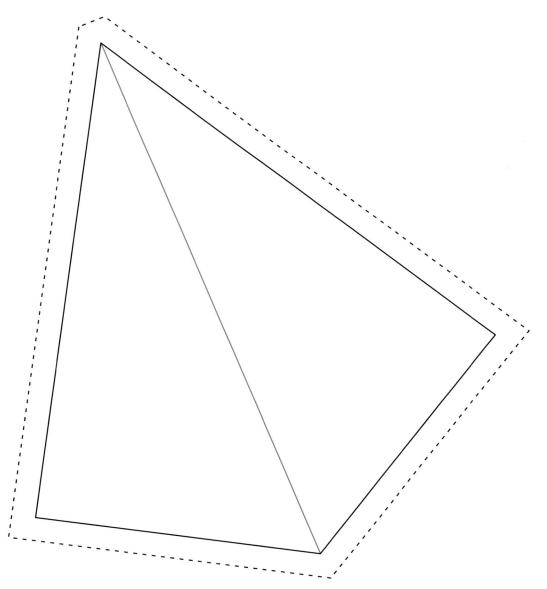

*Make 6 for a 12″ × 10³⁄₈″ block.*
*Add 4 corner triangles using the corner template*
*on page 26 to make the rectangular block.*

# Circle units

Design units are one-fourth the size of a full-size unit.

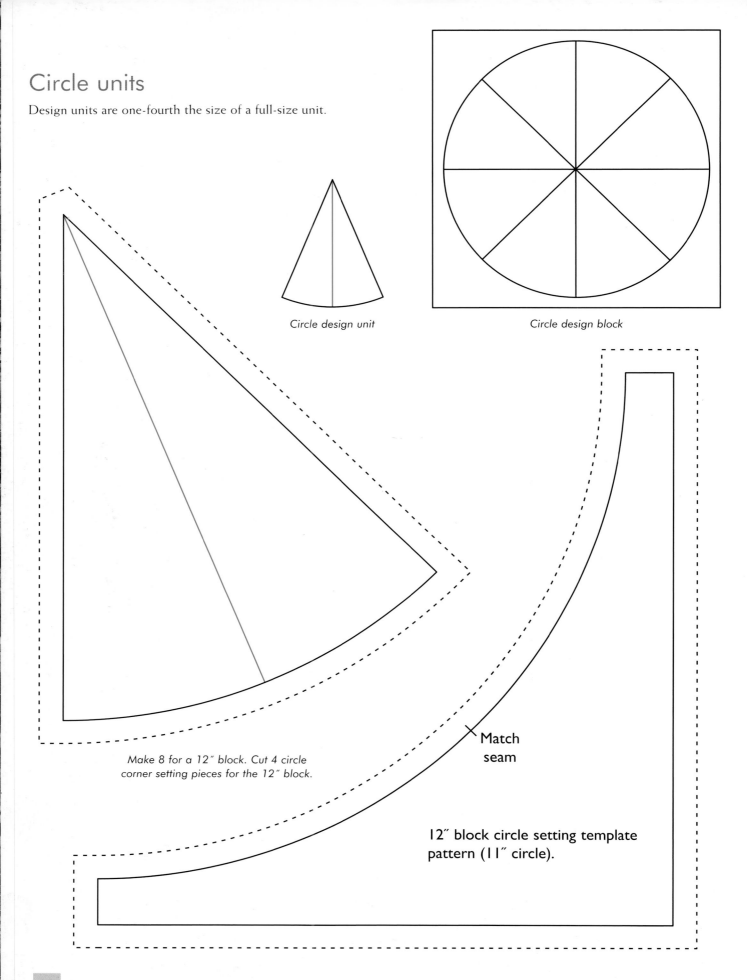

*Circle design unit*

*Circle design block*

*Make 8 for a 12″ block. Cut 4 circle corner setting pieces for the 12″ block.*

Match seam

12″ block circle setting template pattern (11″ circle).

# QUICK-STRIP
# PAPER PIECING
## TECHNIQUE

# Preparation

Before beginning the sewing on your project, you will need to have a few supplies on hand. Most of these are fairly standard sewing supplies and are readily available.

## SUPPLIES

**Rotary cutter, mat, and ruler.** Use these to cut strips for your projects and to square up blocks.

**Sewing machine** with sewing extension table or cabinet. It is possible to use this technique with just a free-arm machine, but having an extension table makes placing the patterns along the strips much easier. Many machines come with these extensions, or they can be ordered for your machine. Having your machine in a cabinet is ideal.

**Open-toe or satin-stitch foot.** This helps you see the needle piercing the sewing line on the paper more easily. If you don't have this type of foot available for your machine, a clear plastic foot works fine, or any foot that lets you see the sewing line.

**Sewing machine needles.** Size 90/14 or 80/12 quilting, jeans/denim, or sharps are my preferred needles for paper piecing. Universal needles also work fine. Do not use a ball-point needle, or a needle designed for knit fabrics. For machine appliqué, use size 70/10 or 75/11 needles.

**Neutral sewing thread.** Use thread that will blend in with the fabrics in your project.

**Spray starch.** Paper piecing often results in block edges being off-grain, and spray starch helps prevent stretching. Spray starch and iron your fabric before or after cutting strips to help prevent distortion when piecing. I find that either regular or heavy spray starch is preferable to fabric sizing. Some people prefer to use liquid starch, which also works well.

**Invisible tape.** This is used to reinforce the paper pattern if you have to rip out and re-sew a line. It is also helpful to "mend" the paper if you accidentally cut it or tear it during the sewing process. Any tape that can be torn easily will work because when the block is finished, the tape needs to be torn away as the paper is removed.

**Paper scissors.** You'll need these to cut out your paper patterns.

**Fabric scissors** of good quality to easily cut across the fabric strips. I prefer sharp 8″ dressmaker's shears, but any shears at least 6″ long are fine. Save small embroidery scissors for the clipping of threads.

**Seam ripper.** Have one on hand just in case you need to un-sew! Use a good sharp one with a tiny point.

**Freezer paper.** Use this for making templates for hexagon and circle settings, and for the curved border patterns.

**Gluestick.** Glue can be used for basting curved borders.

## FABRIC SELECTION

**Fiber content.** I prefer to sew with 100% cotton. That is what most of my stash is made up of, and I know this fabric will behave well in quilts during sewing, pressing, and laundering. However, with paper piecing, the paper provides a foundation while sewing, so other types of fabric such as silks, corduroys, or metallics can also be used. Just take care if they need special treatment when ironing or laundering. If you are using fibers other than cotton, be sure to experiment with a sample of the fabric first to see how it will behave.

I prefer to prewash my cotton fabrics, then spray starch them well before cutting strips. Sometimes, however, I know people prefer to work with fabric without prewashing. That's fine, too—just be sure the colors in your fabric won't run or bleed and that the fabric won't give you any other surprises as you are working with it. Test for colorfastness, or do a small sample first to avoid later problems.

**Styles of prints.** Fabrics that read as solid, mottled fabrics, tone-on-tone fabrics, or small prints all work well. I find that having the fabric read as one particular **value** is often more important than what the print actually is. When the area to be covered is very narrow, or when you want a point to stand out well against the background, be sure to use these types of prints.

Larger-scale prints can be used for spontaneity and excitement. They can be unpredictable, especially if the print has many different colors and values within it. I generally use them in larger areas of a design, where they will have a chance to work well.

I love experimenting with directional fabrics and stripes. These work best in areas where the strip will always be placed at a similar angle. Some blocks can look too chaotic if a stripe is used as the background. But the movement that stripes produce can be quite exciting and can give an otherwise plain block some pizzazz. My favorite places for stripes are at the centers of stars or as backgrounds in circle blocks.

## COPYING PATTERNS

Every block and quilt project in this book is made up of several identical design units that are repeated to form the pattern. You will need a paper pattern for each of these units. Each project will tell you how many copies of the pattern to make for that particular quilt. There are several different ways you can make copies of the patterns.

**Photocopies using a printer/copier or copy machine.** This is the method I prefer to use, because I make many, many copies! I have a printer/copier at home attached to my computer. My printer functions just like a copy machine. I simply lay the pattern on the bed of the machine and it makes a photocopy. Some machines will require you to scan the pattern first, through your computer, and then make a copy. You can also go to a copy shop to make copies. Whatever type of machine you use, hold the first copy up to the original in the book, or your own original pattern, to check the accuracy before making more copies. If the copy varies from the original, try a different machine or adjust the zoom slightly. You want the copies to be accurate if your blocks are to be accurate!

When copying at home, I use 18-pound (when I can find it) or 20-pound copy paper. The 20-pound weight is readily available at most office supply stores and is often recycled paper and therefore quite reasonably priced. You can also

use special paper made just for foundation piecing (it looks like newsprint) that is a little lighter in weight, or vellum, which is translucent. Both are available at quilt stores (see Resources). Most copy shops require you to use whatever paper they have in their machines, which can be a bit heavy for piecing. It never hurts to ask, however, if you can use your own lighter-weight paper in their copy machines.

> *tip*
>
> *Many of the patterns in the book are small enough that two patterns can fit on one sheet of paper. Before making multiple copies of a pattern, make two copies first, check for accuracy, and cut **around** each pattern (outside the lines). Tape or glue them to a sheet of paper and then make the rest of the copies. You'll save paper and money by making two copies at once on each sheet of paper!*

**Tracing copies.** Copies can be traced by hand with a ruler. (Yes, I have some students who prefer to do it that way!) One of my students finds this process quite relaxing, and does it during her TV news time. Again, make sure copies are accurate.

**Sewing machine copies.** Trace or photocopy one accurate copy of the pattern and staple it to several layers of lightweight copy paper or newsprint. With the thread and bobbin removed from your sewing machine, stitch on all the inside and outside lines of the pattern. Hold the pattern sandwich up to the light to make sure you have perforated all the lines. Then remove the staples and transfer the numbers and markings to each pattern using a permanent pen.

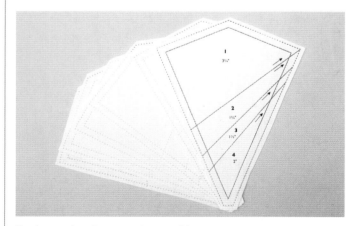

*Copies made using a sewing machine*

## CUTTING OUT THE PATTERNS

Once the patterns are made, cut them out on the outer dashed lines using paper scissors or a rotary cutter with an old blade. The patterns in this book include the ¼″ seam allowances, and I recommend that you use the patterns that way, at least until you master the Quick-Strip Paper Piecing technique. Some quilters prefer to piece their patterns without the seam allowance, to help reduce bulk when sewing patterns together. Once you are confident using the Quick-Strip Paper Piecing technique, feel free to cut out the patterns on the solid outside lines (without seam allowances) before you begin piecing. If you prefer to cut off the seam allowances, remember to leave at least ½″ between the patterns as you place them on the strip, and be careful to include the seam allowances when you are cutting the units apart and trimming them.

## Quick-Strip Paper Piecing

I tried to design patterns for this technique that are easy to use and as mistake-proof as possible. The patterns have some special markings to help you as you use them. See the Star Dance pattern below for an explanation of what the lines and numbers on the pattern mean.

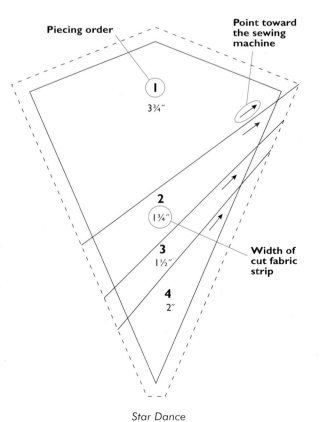

*Star Dance*

The large bold numbers indicate the piecing order—the order in which the strips will be sewn (in this example, from 1 to 4).

**Numbers with inch marks (″) indicate the width of the fabric strip to cut for that area.** For example, in the Star Dance block, the strip size for area 1 is 3¾″. The number of strips you will need to cut for each project is included in the cutting chart for that particular project.

**An arrow in each area points toward the sewing machine** to help you position the paper pattern correctly on the strip.

## SEWING GUIDELINES

**Always keep seam allowances to the right.** This is the way we normally sew seams, so it should be easy to remember. The patterns are designed to be used in this way, with the arrows on the pattern positioned to work with the seam allowances on the right.

**Arrows in the area you are sewing point away from you, toward the sewing machine.** Think of shooting an arrow; you will always point it **away** from you. This helps you position the pattern correctly. With the arrow pointing toward the sewing machine, the new area you are adding (the next higher number) will always be to the right of the needle, with the lower numbers you have already sewn to the left.

## CUTTING FABRIC STRIPS

The width of the fabric strip needed for each area of a pattern is indicated on the pattern and in the cutting chart for each project as well. The project charts will also tell you how many strips you need to cut for that particular project. These numbers are based on strips that are cut from selvage to selvage, approximately 40″ long. Fat quarters certainly can be used, but I find that it is much easier and provides a more efficient use of fabric if strips are cut from selvage to selvage whenever possible. The strip width indicated on the pattern is the **minimum** size strip that will work; if you have strips left over from another project that are larger, they can be used without trimming them down. You can also use strips that are not cut precisely; just make sure you have one side of the strip that is straight, and sew with the seam allowance on the straight side.

## SEWING PREPARATION

**Prepare your sewing machine.** Insert a new size 90/14 or 80/12 needle. My preferred needles are quilting, jeans/denim, or sharps, but universal needles are fine, too.

Set the stitch length shorter than normal, about 16 to 18 stitches per inch, or 1.5 to 1.75mm. This shorter stitch length helps perforate the paper, making paper removal easier, and also strengthens the seam so it won't tear when the paper is removed.

**Cover your ironing surface with a light-colored piece of fabric, such as muslin.** This will absorb any ink that might transfer from the photocopied patterns. Take care because the ink can also be transferred onto any other surface, such as your project, your iron, or your ironing board cover. If ink gets on your iron, be sure to clean it thoroughly with a soft damp cloth before ironing your project!

**Use a dry iron.** Steam will cause your paper to wilt and curl, and a drop of water on the photocopied pattern could also cause the ink to run, so a dry iron is a must!

## PIECING

Following are step-by-step instructions for piecing one Star Dance block with the Quick-Strip Paper Piecing method. The same steps apply for all other blocks in this book.

**1.** Make 8 copies of the Star Dance block on page 46. Cut out the patterns on the outer seamlines.

**2.** Spray starch your fabric. Cut 1 strip of fabric for each area of the block as follows:

Area 1: Cut 1 strip 3¾″ (background fabric).

Area 2: Cut 1 strip 1¾″.

Area 3: Cut 1 strip 1½″.

Area 4: Cut 1 strip 2″.

**3.** Strip 1 and strip 2 will always be added at the same time. Place strip 1 and strip 2 right sides together, **with strip 1 on top**. Align the raw edges on the right side, just as if you were going to sew a normal seam. Place the strips on your sewing machine throatplate as if you were going to sew them with a ¼″ seam. You can even lower the needle at the ¼″ spot if you like.

**4.** The first line on the pattern to sew is the line between areas 1 and 2. Position the pattern so the arrows in 1 and 2 point away from you, **toward** the sewing machine. (Area 1 will be to the left and area 2 to the right.) Looking at the fabric strips on the machine throatplate, visualize where the ¼″ seam will be. Lay the pattern on the fabric strips so that the sewing line falls on the ¼″ seamline.

**5.** Sew on the drawn line of the first pattern, from edge to edge of the paper. When you reach the end of the line, lay the next pattern along the strips in the same manner, and sew the line on that pattern piece. Continue down the strip, adding the pattern pieces until all 8 have been sewn. Make sure the fabric strips stay aligned on the right edge as you sew.

**6.** Remove the sewn strips from the sewing machine. Open out fabric strip 2 from strip 1. Flip the strips over so that the paper units are on top, making sure strip 2 stays opened. Cut the units apart with scissors, following the angle of the paper. Make sure there is enough fabric to cover each area, including a ¼″ seam allowance.

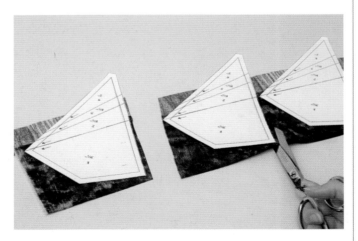

**7.** From the fabric side, press strip 2 open, using a dry iron on the protected ironing surface.

**8.** Trim away excess fabric that hangs over the edge of the paper. There is no need to trim **exactly** on the edge; I prefer to leave a **tiny** bit of fabric showing as I'm piecing the next steps. This helps ensure that the fabric hasn't flipped back and is fully covering the area.

**9.** Lay strip 3 **right side up** on the throatplate. Position the pattern so that the arrow in area 3 points away from you, **toward** the sewing machine. Find the line between area 2 and area 3 and position the paper pattern so the line is ¼″ from the right raw edge of the strip. Sew across the line. Place and sew the other 7 units in the same way.

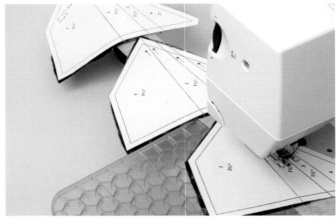

**10.** Remove the sewn units from the machine. Open out strip 3 and cut the units apart, just as you did in Step 6.

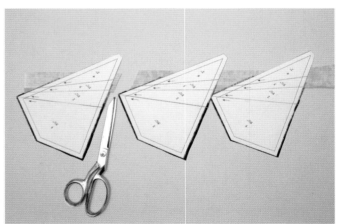

**11.** For every strip added after 1 and 2, there will be excess fabric in the seam allowances. With the fabric side facing toward you, fold the paper away from behind the seam and crease the paper so it stays out of the way.

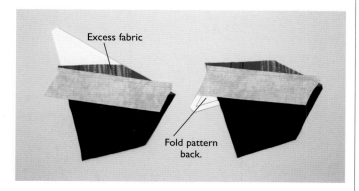

**12.** Using scissors (or a rotary cutter, if you prefer), trim the excess fabric to a ¼˝ seam allowance. Unfold the paper pattern so it is again flat.

**13.** Press open strip 3 on all units. Trim away excess fabric that extends beyond the outer edge of the paper.

**14.** Follow Steps 9 through 12 to add strip 4. When cutting the units apart, be sure to allow enough fabric to completely cover area 4 plus the ¼˝ seam allowance.

**15.** When all fabric strips have been added, use a rotary cutter and ruler to precisely trim the ¼˝ seamline around all the edges. If you have starched your fabric, the paper can be removed now, or you can wait and remove the paper later. See the section on page 37 for suggestions on removing paper.

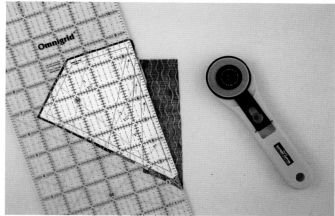

**16.** Follow the instructions for your particular project for assembling the block units, or if you prefer to finish a 12˝ block at this point, cut 2 squares 4½˝ (from background fabric or fabric of your choice), then cut each once on the diagonal for the 4 corner triangles. Sew the 8 pattern units into pairs, pressing the seams either to one side or open. Join 2 pairs into 2 groups of 4 units and press. Sew the 4-unit groups together. You might want to press the last seam open to avoid bulk. Add corner triangles to make the block. The corner triangles are slightly oversized, so just center them and sew. Press the seam toward the triangle, and square up the block to 12½˝.

## MATCHING POINTS

The Star Dance block that was just illustrated doesn't have any points that need to match when the units are sewn together. Many blocks, however, will have points that need to be matched during construction. I use two different pinning methods.

**Method 1. Positioning pin.** I use this first method most often when I leave the paper in during construction, but it can also be used if you have removed the paper first. Place a positioning pin through the point where the two units need to match, leave it in the vertical position, and carefully pin on either side of the positioning pin. The vertical pin can then be removed before sewing.

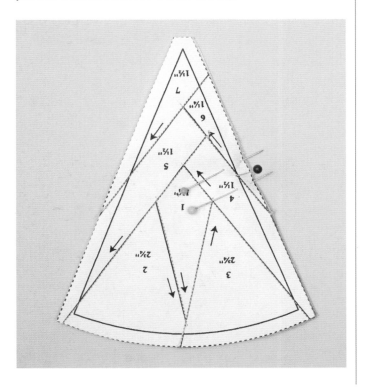

**Method 2. Pinch, peek, and pin.** This is my favorite method for matching points, and I use it most often when I have removed the paper before construction, but it can also be used if you have left the paper in. Line up the two units that will be sewn together. Pinch an inch or so above where the points need to match. Open up the units and peek inside to see that the folds of the two points exactly match. If they don't, wiggle the units a little until the folds match, and pinch to hold in place. Carefully place a pin next to your pinching fingers to hold the units in position. If I use extra-fine pins, I sometimes leave the pins in when I baste the seam.

## BASTING THE POINTS

Sew a few large basting stitches on the ¼″ seamline, just in the areas where the points need to match. If you have more than one point to baste, just lift the presser foot and slide down to the next area you need to match; there is no need to baste the entire seam.

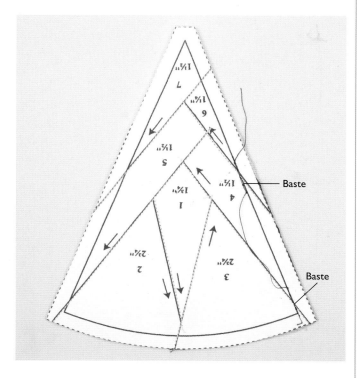

Open out the two units and check the matching points on the front. If the points look good, go ahead and sew the seams, sewing right over the basting stitches. If the points don't match exactly, it is easy to remove the few basting stitches and try again.

## REMOVING THE PAPER

Most people prefer to leave the paper in until the block has been sewn into the quilt. This helps ensure that the off-grain edges won't stretch or distort. However, I have found that I prefer to remove the paper before then, usually after I have finished paper piecing the units and before the units are sewn together into a block. If I have spray starched the fabric well, and if I handle the fabric carefully and take care not to stretch the edges, I find this method works best for me. My students are about evenly divided between those who like to remove the paper as soon as possible and those who like to leave it in until the blocks and top are assembled. I suggest you try both ways and see which works best for you. If your machine tends to stretch the fabric as you piece, you will probably prefer to leave the paper in as long as possible.

To remove the paper, **begin with the last seam sewn**. Fold and crease on the stitching line, then carefully tear the paper away, supporting the seam with the fingers of your other hand as you tear the paper. This is most easily accomplished by working on a flat surface, such as a tabletop or lapboard, to help prevent stretching and distortion of the fabric. If you remove the paper before sewing the units together, begin with the highest number on the unit, then work backward down to number 1. If you have waited until your blocks have been sewn together, that means you will begin removing the paper from the seam allowances first, and then continue on to each unit, starting with the highest number.

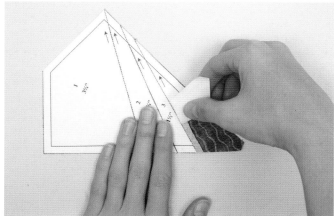

## PATTERNS WITH INDENTED LINES

Blocks such as Star Dance and Palm Leaf have lines that completely cross the block from edge to edge, making them the easiest to sew using the Quick-Strip Paper Piecing technique. Some other patterns in the book have indented lines that begin or end somewhere in the middle of the block. Compare the Star Dance pattern with the Evening Star pattern.

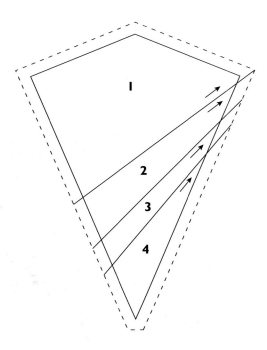

*Star Dance—all sewing lines extend from edge to edge.*

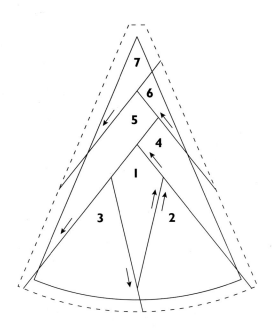

*Evening Star—all sewing lines but one are indented.*

## SEWING TIPS FOR INDENTED LINES

■ Place the pattern where you think the ¼″ seam will fall, then lift the paper and check for the ¼″ seam by peeking underneath to see if it is placed properly. You can lower the presser foot or the needle onto the paper and fabric before peeking to help keep the pattern in place.

■ When beginning with an indented line, sew 2 to 3 stitches before the beginning of the drawn line to lock the stitches. Do the same thing if the end of the line is indented—simply sew a few stitches beyond the line.

■ After sewing the first pattern, place the next pattern on the strip. Lift the presser foot and slide the strip away from you to begin sewing on the next pattern. Stitch as before, beginning and ending a few stitches beyond the indented line. It is all right if the patterns overlap in areas that aren't involved in the seam; just be sure the area you are sewing has sufficient fabric on the strip to cover that area plus a ¼″ seam allowance.

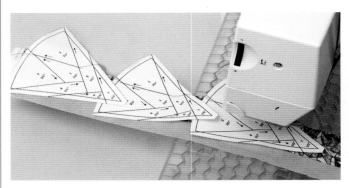

■ When cutting units apart, be sure you leave enough fabric to completely cover the area you are adding, plus the ¼″ seam allowance.

■ Sometimes you may feel you are wasting too much of the strip if the indented line is a long way from the edge of the paper. The paper can be folded out of the way to save strip space—just be sure you are not shorting any points or other spots in the area you are adding. Remember that you must cover the area **plus** the ¼″ seam allowance all around it.

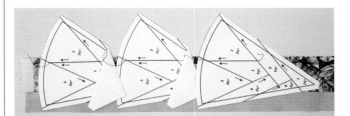

## CORRECTING MISTAKES

We all make mistakes from time to time. If you need to rip out a seam, use a good sharp seam ripper, or a tiny scissors. Here are two different methods for "un-sewing":

**Method 1.** Rip out the seam on the fabric side to avoid tearing the paper. Lift the fabric strip up and cut the stitches in between the two fabric layers with your seam ripper. Tug gently on the strip to rip the next stitch or two, then use your seam ripper again to break the next set of stitches. If you find that it is almost impossible to remove the stitches, set your stitch length just a little bit longer. If your paper is weakened after the removal of a seam, place a piece of invisible tape over the seamline on the lined side of the paper. Tape can also be used to mend the paper if you accidentally cut the paper at any point in the construction process.

**Method 2.** Another way to rip out a seam is to first place a piece of tape over the paper on the line you will rip out. Carefully tear the sewn fabric away from the paper, trying not to rip the paper. Then rip out the seam as you would any other seam.

# PROJECTS

# STAR **DANCE**

*Star Dance,* by Peggy Martin, 2003. Quilt size: 37″ × 37″.

The Star Dance block is a simple block with a lot of movement and design potential. It is one of the easiest blocks to sew using the Quick-Strip Paper Piecing technique, and is great for beginners.

## Selecting fabrics

I chose jewel tones of blue, green, and fuchsia, inspired by the border print I had selected. I chose mostly tone-on-tone prints, which read as solids or mottled solids, and one busy multicolored print and one stripe for the star centers.

## Fabrics

Dark blue
(includes binding): 1⅛ yards

Light blue/green: ⅝ yard

Fuchsia: ½ yard

Blue/green stripe: ⅛ yard

Fuchsia/green print: ¼ yard

Wide stripe: ¾ yard

Backing: 1¼ yards

Batting: 42″ × 42″

## Cutting fabrics

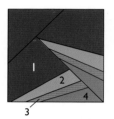

*Star Dance 6″
center squares*

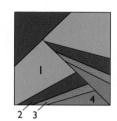

*Star Dance 6″
surrounding squares*

*Note: All strips are cut from selvage to selvage and measure about 40″ long.*

| FABRIC | BLOCK | PATTERN AREA | CUT |
|---|---|---|---|
| Dark blue | Center | 1 | 1 strip 3¾″ |
| | Surrounding | 2 | 3 strips 1¾″ |
| | All | Setting triangles | 8 squares 4½″; cut once diagonally to make 16 triangles |
| | | 1st border | 4 strips 2″ |
| | | Binding | 4 strips 2″ |
| Light blue/green | Center | 2 | 1 strip 1¾″ |
| | Surrounding | 1 | 3 strips 3¾″ |
| Fuchsia | All | 3 | 4 strips 1½″ |
| | | 2nd border | 4 strips 1½″ |
| Blue/green stripe | Center | 4 | 1 strip 2″ |
| Fuchsia/green print | Surrounding | 4 | 3 strips 2″ |
| Wide stripe | | 3rd border | 4 strips 4½″ |

# Copying the pattern

Make 32 copies of the Star Dance pattern on page 46. Cut out the 32 units on the dashed outer seamline.

# Making the quilt

*See pages 29–39 for complete Quick-Strip Paper Piecing instructions.*

**1.** For the center squares, make 8 units as shown using the strips indicated in the chart. Sew the units into 4 pairs. Press the seams to one side (or open if you prefer). Add a setting triangle to each pair, centering the triangle (triangles are slightly oversized). Press the seam toward the triangle, and square up to 6½″.

 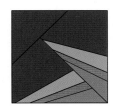

Center unit; make 8.     Center square; make 4.

**2.** For the surrounding squares, make 24 units as shown using the strips indicated in the chart. Sew the units into 12 pairs. Add a setting triangle to each pair, centering the triangle (triangles are slightly oversized). Press the seam toward the triangle, and square up to 6½″.

Surrounding unit;     Surrounding square;
make 24.     make 12.

**3.** Lay out the squares as shown in the Quilt Assembly Diagram. Sew together in rows to make the body of the quilt.

**4.** Measure the quilt, cut the top and bottom first border strips to fit, and sew them to the quilt. Press the seams toward the borders. Repeat for the side first border strips. Add the second and third borders in the same manner.

**5.** I quilted my quilt with swirls and radiating lines to add to the movement of the blocks.

*Quilt Assembly Diagram*

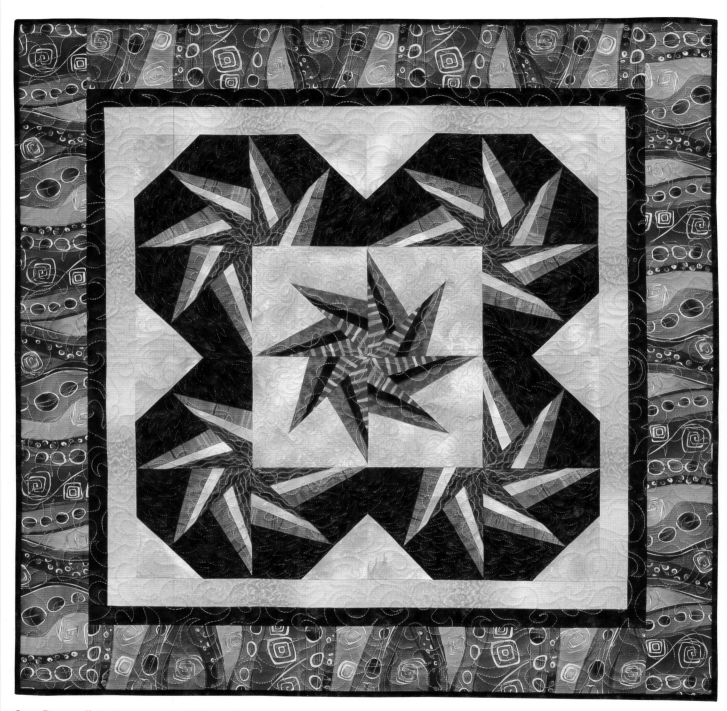

*Star Dance II*, by Peggy Martin, 2003. Quilt size: 35″ × 35″.

This quilt uses the same layout as *Star Dance,* with a different color scheme and the light and dark areas reversed.

*Autumn Dance*, by Peggy Martin, 2005. Quilt size: 67″ × 67″.
Machine quilted by Linda Kamm.

The idea of setting Star Dance blocks with rings of partial
blocks is expanded in this quilt, with multiple rings dancing
around the center star. The rich autumn colors inspired
the title.

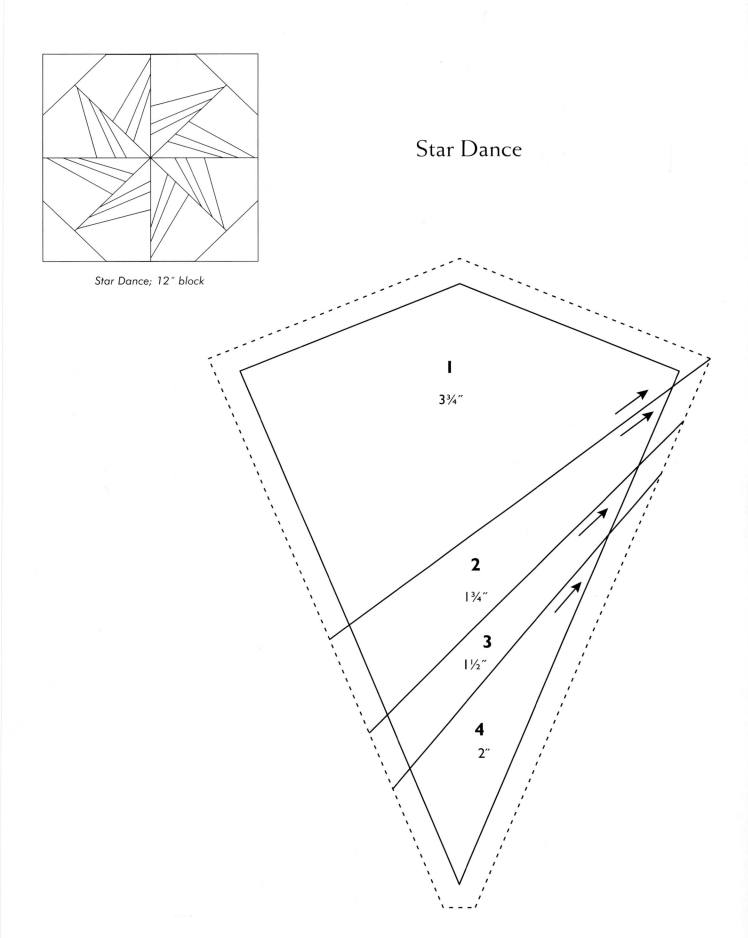

## Star Dance

Star Dance; 12″ block

I

3¾″

2

1¾″

3

1½″

4

2″

# LOOKING **UP**

*Looking Up*, by Sandra McCullough, 2005. Quilt size: 52˝ × 66˝. Machine quilted by Linda Kamm.

This Star Dance lap quilt is set in straight rows with narrow sashing around each block. The Star Dance blocks are sewn quickly and easily—no points to match!

## Selecting fabrics

Sandra chose a selection of beautiful batiks for her star fabrics, making two blocks in each fabric combination. The multicolored border print picks up all the colors in the blocks.

## Fabrics

Taupe batik: 1½ yards

18 assorted batiks in golds, purples, blues, and greens: ⅛ to ¼ yard of **each**

Green batik: ½ yard

Green/purple batik: 1 yard

Gold batik (includes binding): ¾ yard

Green/purple/gold batik: 1⅛ yards

Backing: 3⅛ yards

Batting: 57″ × 71″

## Cutting fabrics

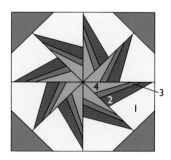

Star Dance; 12″ block

| FABRIC | PATTERN AREA | CUT |
|---|---|---|
| Taupe batik | 1 | 12 strips 3¾″ |
| 18 assorted batiks | 2 | 2 strips 1¾″ of each of 6 different batiks |
|  | 3 | 2 strips 1½″ of each of 6 different batiks |
|  | 4 | 2 strips 2″ of each of 6 different batiks |
| Green batik | Corner triangles | 24 squares 4½″; cut once diagonally to make 48 triangles |
| Green/purple batik | Sashing | 20 strips 1½″; cut into 24 strips 12½″ long and 24 strips 14½″ long |
| Gold batik | Folded border | 5 strips 1″ |
|  | Binding | 6 strips 2″ |
| Green/purple/gold batik | Outer border | 6 strips 5½″ |

*Note: All strips are cut from selvage to selvage and measure about 40″ long.*

## ▩ Copying the pattern

Make 96 copies of the Star Dance pattern on page 46. Cut out the 96 units on the dashed outer seam line.

## ▩ Making the quilt

*See pages 29–39 for complete Quick-Strip Paper Piecing instructions.*

**1.** Make 2 blocks at a time by sewing 16 identical units from each fabric combination, using the strips indicated in the chart. Sew the units into 8 pairs. Press the seams to one side (or open if you prefer). Join the pairs into block halves, then join the halves to make 2 blocks.

**2.** Add setting triangles to the 4 corners of each block, centering the triangles (triangles are slightly oversized). Press the seam toward the triangle, and square up the blocks to 12½˝.

**3.** Make 6 sets of 2 blocks for a total of 12 blocks.

*Make 12 blocks.*

**4.** Sew 12½˝-long sashing strips to 2 opposite sides of each block; press toward the sashing. Sew 14½˝-long sashing strips to the remaining sides; press toward the sashing.

**5.** Sew the blocks together in rows and then sew the rows together following the Quilt Assembly Diagram.

**6.** Add the folded border.

**a.** Sew together the five 1˝ gold border strips with diagonal seams as follows: place 2 strips right sides together, at right angles, with a bit of each strip hanging beyond the intersection. Sew across the intersection of the strips. Join the next strip to the end of the first 2 strips, adding on each strip until you have made 1 long continuous strip.

Trim the seam allowances on the diagonal seams to ¼˝ and press the seams open.

*Sewing diagonal seams*

**b.** Fold the strip in half along the length, and press. Cut the strips to fit the top, align the raw edges of the strips with the raw edges of the quilt top, and sew the folded strips to the quilt top with a **scant** ¼˝ seam. Sew strips to the top and bottom of the quilt first, then sew strips to the sides, overlapping the strips at the corners. Do not open out the strips, but leave them lying with the folded edges toward the center of the quilt.

**7.** Measure the quilt, piece the border strips end to end as necessary, and cut the top and bottom border strips to fit. Place the outer border on top of the folded border, matching the edge of the quilt. Sew the top and bottom outer borders to the quilt with a ¼˝ seam allowance. Press the seams toward the borders. Add the side borders in the same manner.

**8.** *Looking Up* was quilted with floral and leafy vine patterns in the taupe background and swirls in the stars. Floral motifs were repeated in the border.

*Quilt Assembly Diagram*

*Tutti Frutti,* by Yvonne Regala, 2005. Quilt size: 46″ × 57″. Machine quilted by Faith Horsky.

Yvonne simplified the Star Dance pattern by eliminating one of the piecing lines in the star and using a striped fabric for that larger area. The blocks were made with lots of fun, bright fabrics left over from another project.

***Light Up the Fourth,*** by Lorraine Marstall, 2005. Quilt size: 54″ x 54″.

This is a tribute to the many years of trekking with family and friends to ooh and ah at fireworks on the Fourth of July. Lorraine set her Star Dance blocks without sashing and designed the border pattern by drafting a mirror image of the Star Dance pattern, then sewing the original pattern and mirror image together. The border corners were simplified by eliminating some lines.

# CHRISTMAS CACTUS

*Christmas Cactus,* by Peggy Martin, 2004. Quilt size: 32″ × 32″.

*Christmas Cactus* is a wall quilt made from the Palm Leaf block. I colored the block with green in the larger points and red in the two smallest points. This made it look more like a flower than a palm leaf, and reminded me of the Christmas cactus plant. There are many ways Palm Leaf blocks can be arranged for entirely different looks. Be sure to play with your blocks a bit before you sew them together to find the design you like best.

## Selecting fabrics

I chose a buttery cream color for the background. I used 16 different greens in varying shades for the leaves and 8 different reds for the flowers. I divided these into 4 sets of fabrics: 2 reds and 4 greens for each set. I cut 1 strip of each fabric and made 4 identical blocks from each set. There was quite a bit of fabric left over on several of the strips using this scrappy approach. The yardage below reflects the minimum number of strips needed.

## Fabrics

Cream background: 1¼ yards

Assorted green fabrics: ¾ yard total

Assorted red fabrics: ⅜ yard total

Border and binding: 1 yard

Backing: 1⅛ yards

Batting: 37″ × 37″

## Cutting fabrics

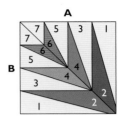

*Palm Leaf; 6″ block*

| FABRIC | PATTERN AREA | CUT |
|---|---|---|
| Background | 1, 3, 5, 7 | 18 strips 2¼″ |
| Assorted greens | 2, 4 | 12 strips 2″ (total) |
| Assorted reds | 6 | 4 strips 2″ |
| Red and green print | Border | 4 strips 4½″ |
| | Binding | 4 strips 2″ |

*Note: All strips are cut from selvage to selvage and measure about 40″ long.*

# Copying the patterns

Make 16 copies of Palm Leaf pattern A and 16 copies of Palm Leaf pattern B on page 58. Cut out the 32 units on the dashed outer seamlines.

# Making the quilt

*See pages 29–39 for complete Quick-Strip Paper Piecing instructions.*

**1.** Make 16 of unit A and 16 of unit B using the strips indicated in the chart.

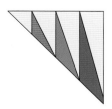

*A units; make 16.*

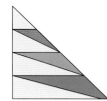

*B units; make 16.*

**2.** Sew units A and B together, in pairs, matching up points. Press the seams open for less bulk.

*Make 16.*

**3.** Lay out the squares as shown in the Quilt Assembly Diagram, or rearrange them as you like to form a new design. Sew the blocks together in rows, then sew the rows together to make the body of the quilt.

**4.** Measure the quilt and cut the top and bottom border strips to fit. Sew the borders to the quilt. Press the seams toward the borders. Add the side borders in the same manner.

**5.** I quilted my quilt with gently curving lines in the flower sections and stippling in the background.

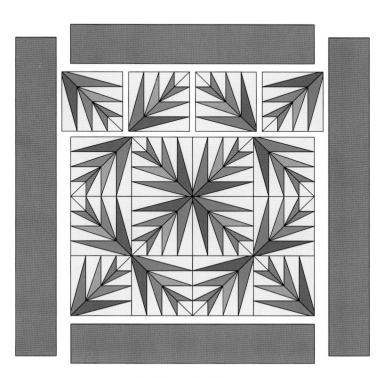

*Quilt Assembly Diagram*

*Farewell to Indian Summer,* by Jean Nagy, 2005. Quilt size: 30″ × 30″.

The Palm Leaf block works very well as a border. In *Farewell to Indian Summer,* Jean Nagy chose to surround her appliquéd birdhouse and Broderie Perse autumn leaves with a border of Palm Leaf blocks.

*One Hour to Expire,* by Mary Tabar, 2005. Quilt size: 31½″ × 42″.
Machine quilted by Linda Kamm.

Mary Tabar used various sizes of Palm Leaf blocks by shrinking the pattern on a copy machine. She experimented with dyeing her fabrics by adding them to the dye bath at different times, until the dye bath had completely expired, producing much lighter colors. The blocks swirl around the center of the quilt, getting smaller and lighter as they approach the smallest square near the center, which is actually cut out of the quilt.

# Palm Leaf

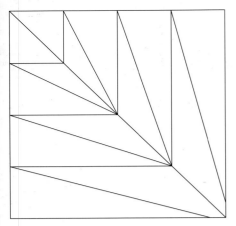

*Palm Leaf; 6″ block*

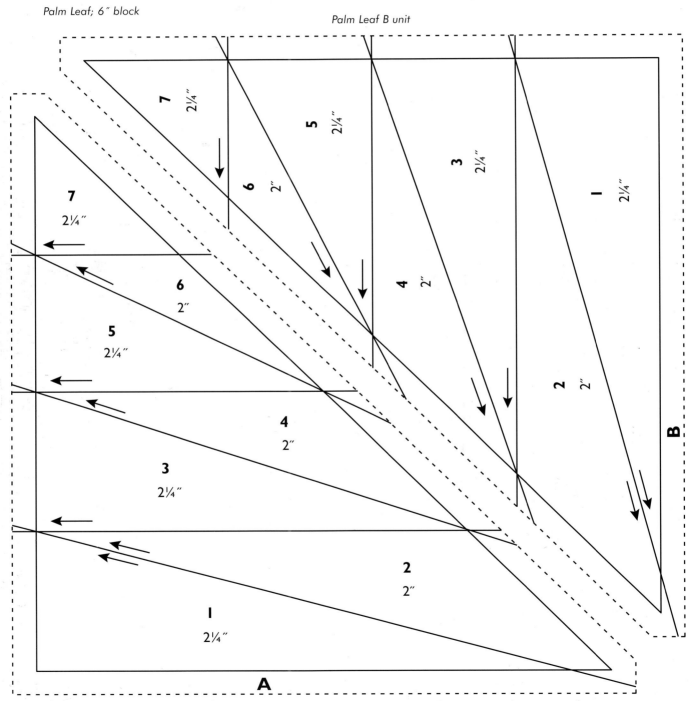

*Palm Leaf B unit*

**7**
2¼″

**5**
2¼″

**3**
2¼″

**I**
2¼″

**6**
2″

**4**
2″

**2**
2″

**B**

**7**
2¼″

**6**
2″

**5**
2¼″

**4**
2″

**3**
2¼″

**2**
2″

**I**
2¼″

**A**

*Palm Leaf A unit*

# CACTUS TREE

*Cactus Tree*, by Peggy Martin, 2004. Quilt size: 51˝ × 65˝.

Positive/negative design elements have always intrigued me. The Palm Leaf pattern, with its mirror-image design, seemed a natural choice to use in a positive/negative design. Four Palm Leaf units are rotated to produce a 12″ block with points radiating out from the center.

## Selecting fabrics

This is a scrap quilt, with each block different. There are 2 fabrics in each block, alternated in a positive/negative design. I used 24 different bright fabrics and experimented with different types of prints in this quilt. I wanted it to be lively and fun, so I used busy prints in some of the blocks. The blocks with busier prints have a much lower contrast, and the points don't stand out as well. More solid-looking fabrics had a higher contrast and showed the design better.

## Fabrics

12 different darks: ³⁄₈ yard of **each**

12 different lights: ³⁄₈ yard of **each**

Assorted brights for sashing: 1 yard total

Large print for border: 1 yard

Binding: ½ yard

Backing: 3⅛ yards

Batting: 56″ × 70″

## Cutting fabrics

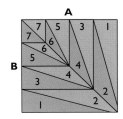

*Palm Leaf; 6″ block*

| FABRIC | PATTERN AREA | CUT |
|---|---|---|
| 12 dark fabrics | A: 1, 3, 5, 7 | 2 strips 2¼″ of each |
|  | B: 2, 4, 6 | 2 strips 2″ of each |
| 12 light fabrics | A: 2, 4, 6 | 2 strips 2″ of each |
|  | B: 1, 3, 5, 7 | 2 strips 2¼″ of each |
| Bright fabrics for sashing | Sashing strips | 18–20 strips 1½″; cut into 24 strips 12½″ long and 24 strips 14½″ long |
| Large print | Border | 6 strips 5″ |
| Binding fabric | Binding | 6 strips 2″ |

*Note: All strips are cut from selvage to selvage and measure about 40″ long.*

## Copying the patterns

Make 48 copies of Palm Leaf pattern A and 48 copies of Palm Leaf pattern B on page 58. Cut out the patterns.

# Making the quilt

*See pages 29–39 for complete Quick-Strip Paper Piecing instructions.*

**1.** From **each** of the 12 fabric combinations, make 4 of unit A and 4 of unit B (a total of 48 of A and 48 of B) using the strips indicated in the chart.

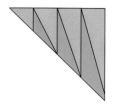 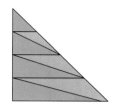

*A units; make 4 of **each** of the 12 fabric combinations.*    *B units; make 4 of **each** of the 12 fabric combinations.*

**2.** For each color combination, sew units A and B together in pairs, matching up points. Press the seams open for less bulk. Join the 4 pairs together in each color combination to form 12 blocks. Press the seams open.

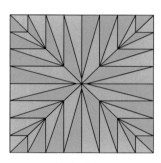

*Make 12.*

**3.** Using the various bright sashing strips, sew 12½"-long strips to 2 opposite sides of each block, and press toward the sashing. Sew 14½"-long strips to the remaining sides, and press toward the sashing. Vary the colors around the blocks as you desire.

**4.** Lay out the blocks as shown in the Quilt Assembly Diagram. Sew the blocks together in rows, then sew the rows together to make the body of the quilt.

**5.** Measure the quilt, piece the border strips as necessary, and cut the top and bottom border strips to fit the quilt. Sew the borders to the quilt. Press the seams toward the borders. Add the side borders in the same manner.

**6.** I quilted my quilt with squiggles in the points of the blocks and loops in the sashing. I used a feather quilting design in the border.

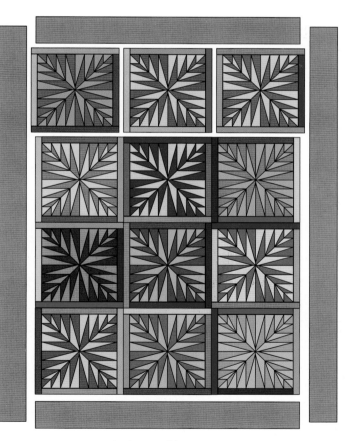

*Quilt Assembly Diagram*

*Tequila Star Rise*, by Allegra ("Lee") Olson, 2005. Quilt size: 42″ × 54″.

The Wishing Star block was designed using half-square triangles that are mirror imaged to produce an elongated star. In this lively lap quilt, portions of blocks are used as borders to frame the center of the quilt.

## ❋ Selecting fabrics

Lee chose a burnished gold as the background to set off the saturated blues and reds in the star points. The center blocks are done in reds and blues on the gold background, while the border blocks are done just in blue fabrics on the same gold background. Tone-on-tone, mottled, or subtle prints were selected.

## ❋ Fabrics

Gold: 2⅝ yards

Light blue: ¾ yard

Medium blue: 1 yard

Dark red: ½ yard

Medium red: ½ yard

Dark blue (includes border and binding): 1⅞ yards

Backing: 2¾ yards

Batting: 47″ × 59″

## ❋ Cutting fabrics

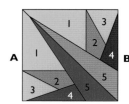

Wishing Star;
6″ center square

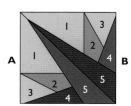

Wishing Star;
6″ border square

*Note: All strips are cut from selvage to selvage and measure about 40″ long.*

| FABRIC | BLOCK | PATTERN AREA | CUT |
|---|---|---|---|
| Gold | All | A1 and B1 | 12 strips 4¾″ |
| | All | A3 and B3 | 12 strips 2½″ |
| Light blue | All | A2 and B2 | 12 strips 2″ |
| Medium blue | Center | A4 | 4 strips 2″ |
| | Border | B4 | 4 strips 2″ |
| | Border | A5 | 6 strips 2½″ |
| Dark red | Center | A5 | 6 strips 2½″ |
| Medium red | Center | B5 | 6 strips 2½″ |
| Dark blue | Center | B4 | 4 strips 2″ |
| | Border | A4 | 4 strips 2″ |
| | Border | B5 | 6 strips 2½″ |
| | | Outer border | 5 strips 3½″ |
| | | Binding | 6 strips 2″ |

## ✳ Copying the patterns

Make 48 copies each of Wishing Star patterns A and B on page 65. Cut out the patterns on the outer dashed seamlines.

## ✳ Making the quilt

*See pages 29–39 for complete Quick-Strip Paper Piecing instructions.*

**1. Center blocks.** Make 24 A units and 24 B units using the fabrics and strips indicated in the chart. Sew the units into 24 pairs. Press the seams open for the sharpest points.

*Make 24 A units.*          *Make 24 B units.*

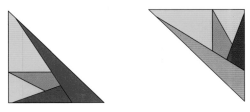

*Sew A and B together; press seams open.*

**2. Border blocks.** Make 24 A units and 24 B units using the fabrics and strips indicated in the chart. Sew the units into 24 pairs. Press the seams open for the sharpest points.

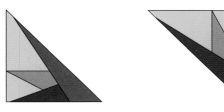

*Make 24 A units.*          *Make 24 B units.*

*Sew A and B together; press seams open.*

**3.** Lay out the squares as shown in the Quilt Assembly Diagram. Sew them together in rows, then sew the rows together to make the body of the quilt.

**4.** Measure the quilt and cut the top and bottom border strips to fit. Sew the borders to the quilt. Press the seams toward the borders. Add the side borders in the same manner.

**5.** Lee quilted the stars in-the-ditch to make them stand out. Star shapes were then quilted in the background and borders to enhance the star theme.

*Quilt Assembly Diagram*

# Wishing Star

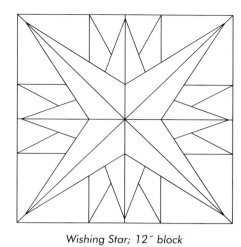

*Wishing Star; 12" block*

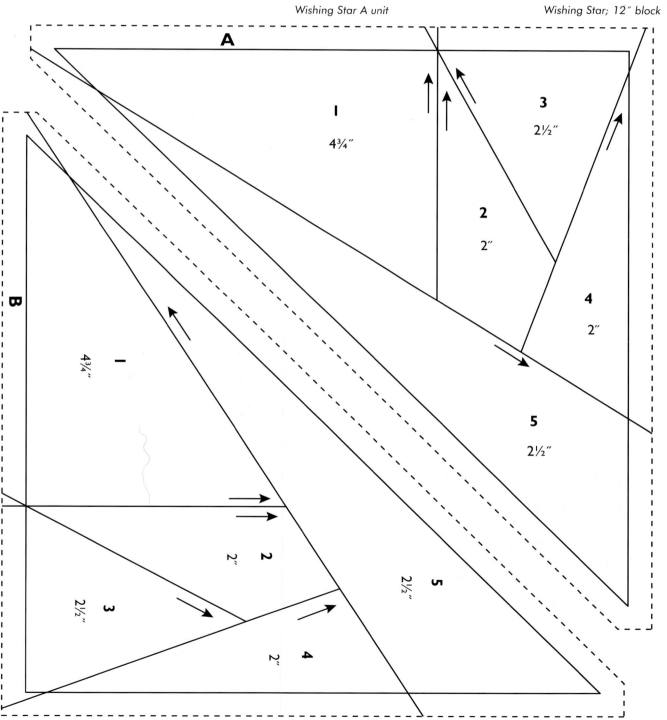

*Wishing Star A unit*

A

**1**

4¾"

**3**

2½"

**2**

2"

**4**

2"

**5**

2½"

B

**1**

4¾"

**2**

2"

**3**

2½"

**4**

2"

**5**

2½"

*Wishing Star B unit*

# STARLIGHT, **STARBRIGHT**

*Starlight, Starbright,* by Patricia Wolfe, 2005. Quilt size: 36″ × 36″.

I originally designed the Wishing Star block to be set on point. This quilt looks like a diagonal set but is actually created by sewing triangle segments in the corners of the blocks to set them on point, making construction easier.

## ✳ Selecting fabrics

Pat selected two different background colors, light and dark blue. She then selected red-orange, yellow, turquoise, and a turquoise and red print for the star points. The bright star fabrics really sparkle against the light and dark blue backgrounds.

## ✳ Fabrics

Light blue: 1¼ yards

Dark blue (includes border and binding): 1⅝ yards

Turquoise and red print: ¾ yard

Turquoise: ½ yard

Yellow: ½ yard

Yellow print: ½ yard

Red-orange: ¾ yard

Backing: 1¼ yards

Batting: 41″ × 41″

## ✳ Cutting fabrics

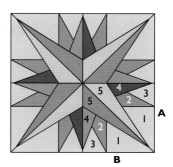

*Wishing Star blocks; 12″ block*

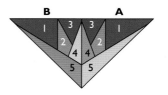

*Wishing Star corners*

*Note: All strips are cut from selvage to selvage and measure about 40″ long.*

| FABRIC | BLOCK | PATTERN AREA | CUT |
|---|---|---|---|
| Light blue | Blocks | A1, B1 | 4 strips 4¾″ |
| | Blocks | A3, B3 | 4 strips 2½″ |
| | Corners | B4 | 2 strips 2″ |
| Dark blue | Blocks | A4 | 2 strips 2″ |
| | Corners | A1, B1 | 4 strips 4¾″ |
| | Corners | A3, B3 | 4 strips 2½″ |
| | Border | | 4 strips 1½″ |
| | Binding | | 4 strips 2″ |
| Turquoise/red print | Blocks | A2, B2 | 4 strips 2″ |
| | Corners | A2, B2 | 4 strips 2″ |
| Turquoise | Blocks | B4 | 2 strips 2″ |
| | Corners | A4 | 2 strips 2″ |
| Yellow | Blocks | A5 | 4 strips 2½″ |
| Yellow print | Corners | A5 | 4 strips 2½″ |
| Red-orange | Blocks and corners | B5 | 8 strips 2½″ |

## ✳ Copying the patterns

Make 32 copies **each** of Wishing Star patterns A and B on page 65. Cut out the patterns on the outer seamlines.

## ✳ Making the quilt

*See pages 29–39 for complete Quick-Strip Paper Piecing instructions.*

**1.** **Center blocks.** Make 16 A units and 16 B units using the fabrics and strips indicated in the chart for blocks. Sew the units into 16 pairs, pressing the seams open. Join the pairs into 4 blocks.

*Make 4 blocks.*

**2.** **Corner triangles.** Make 16 A units and 16 B units using the fabrics and strips indicated in the chart for corners. Sew the units into 16 triangle pairs as shown below. Press the seams open.

*Make 16 corner triangles.*

**3.** Sew corner triangles to the sides of each block.

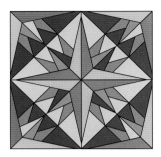

*Make 4.*

**4.** Lay out the blocks as shown in the Quilt Assembly Diagram. Sew the blocks together in rows, then sew the rows together to make the body of the quilt.

**5.** Measure the quilt and cut the top and bottom border strips to fit. Sew the borders to the quilt. Press the seams toward the borders. Add the side borders in the same manner.

**6.** Pat quilted in-the-ditch around all the star points and did heavy background quilting radiating around the star points.

*Quilt Assembly Diagram*

*Starry Glow*, by Annette Friedlein, 2005. Quilt size: 39″ × 39″. Machine quilted by Linda Kamm.

Annette chose the same setting for her Wishing Star blocks but selected brightly colored prints with a lot of movement. Each block is different, with its own distinct personality. The elongated star points were trapuntoed to further enhance the center of the blocks.

*Dusk to Dawn*, by Peggy Martin, 2005. Quilt size: 62½″ × 62½″. Machine quilted by Linda Kamm.

I wanted to set the Wishing Star blocks on point with Palm Leaf triangles in the corners. I chose the Flying Geese setting for the Palm Leaf triangles because it made the star blocks look like they were no longer square, but bowed out on the sides. I also played with a positive/negative design element, alternating between dark and light backgrounds.

## ◈ Selecting fabrics

For the star backgrounds I chose two beautiful batiks, one light and one dark. The light one is pink with areas of yellow and green. The dark batik is burgundy with areas of red-violet and green. The Palm Leaf triangles were made of these two fabrics as well. The Wishing Star blocks are scrappy, using many different pink, purple, and green fabrics.

## ◈ Fabrics

Burgundy batik (includes outer border and binding): 4½ yards

Pink batik (includes inner border): 3¾ yards

Star points: 45 assorted pinks, purples, and greens: ⅛ yard to ¼ yard of **each**

Backing: 3¾ yards

Batting: 67″ × 67″

## ◈ Cutting fabrics

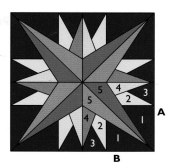

*Wishing Star; 12″ block*

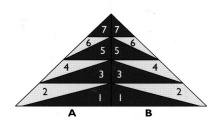

*Palm Leaf corner triangles, 6″ × 12″*

*Note: All strips are cut from selvage to selvage and measure about 40″ long.*

| FABRIC | BLOCK | PATTERN AREA | CUT |
|---|---|---|---|
| Burgundy batik | Wishing Star, dark | A1, B1 | 4 strips 4¾″ |
|  | Wishing Star, dark | A3, B3 | 4 strips 2½″ |
|  | Palm Leaf, dark | A: 1, 3, 5, 7 B: 1, 3, 5, 7 | 18 strips 2¼″ |
|  | Palm Leaf, light | A: 2, 4, 6 B: 2, 4, 6 | 18 strips 2″ |
|  |  | Outer border | 6 strips 5″ |
|  |  | Binding | 7 strips 2″ |
| Pink batik | Wishing Star, light | A1, B1 | 5 strips 4¾″ |
|  | Wishing Star, light | A3, B3 | 5 strips 2½″ |
|  | Palm Leaf, light | A: 1, 3, 5, 7 B: 1, 3, 5, 7 | 21 strips 2¼″ |
|  | Palm Leaf, dark | A: 2, 4, 6 B: 2, 4, 6 | 16 strips 2″ |
|  |  | Inner border | 6 strips 1¾″ |
| 9 assorted colors | Wishing Star, light and dark | A2, B2, A4, B4 | 1 strip 2″ of each |
|  | ″ | A5, B5 | 1 strip 2½″ of each |

# Copying the patterns

Make 36 copies each of Wishing Star patterns A and B on page 65. Make 36 copies each of Palm Leaf patterns A and B on page 58. Cut out the patterns on the outer seamlines.

# Making the quilt

*See pages 29–39 for complete Quick-Strip Paper Piecing instructions.*

**1.** **Wishing Star blocks.** Make 4 dark Wishing Star blocks using the burgundy background and the fabrics and strips indicated in the cutting chart. Each block is made with 4 A and 4 B units. Piece the A and B units and sew them together on the diagonal into pairs, then join the pairs to make the blocks. Press the seams open for the sharpest points.

Make 5 light Wishing Star blocks in the same manner using the pink background and the fabrics and strips indicated in the cutting chart.

 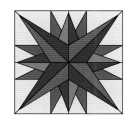

*Wishing Star dark background; make 4.*    *Wishing Star light background; make 5.*

**2.** **Palm Leaf background triangles.** Make 16 A and 16 B dark background Palm Leaf units with pink points using the strips indicated in the cutting chart. Make 20 A and 20 B light background Palm Leaf units with burgundy points using the strips indicated in the cutting chart. Sew the dark units into pairs and the light units into pairs as shown below. Press the seams open for the sharpest points.

*Make 16 dark background triangles.*    *Make 20 light background triangles.*

**3.** **Sew the blocks.** Sew the dark Palm Leaf background triangles to the 4 dark Wishing Star blocks. Sew the light Palm Leaf background triangles to the 5 light Wishing Star blocks.

*Make 4 dark background blocks.*

*Make 5 light background blocks.*

**4.** Lay out the quilt blocks as shown in the Quilt Assembly Diagram. Sew the blocks together in rows, then sew the rows together to make the body of the quilt.

**5.** Measure the quilt and cut the top and bottom inner border strips to fit. Sew the borders to the quilt. Press the seams toward the borders. Add the inner side borders in the same manner. Repeat for the outer border.

**6.** Linda Kamm quilted my quilt with free-form swirls and flame shapes in the backgrounds and borders, adding even more movement to the quilt design.

*Quilt Assembly Diagram*

*Night Fire,* by Peggy Martin, 2005. Quilt size: 47" × 47".

*Night Fire* is a medallion quilt with a central Wishing Star block set on point, and Palm Leaf triangles in the Sawtooth setting for the corners and borders. As I worked on this quilt, I envisioned the image of flames burning over the ridges of hills at night—an image burned into my memory from the devastating firestorms we experienced in San Diego in October 2003.

## ◈ Selecting fabrics

Black with brights has always been a favorite color scheme of mine. In *Night Fire*, I used several different black print backgrounds and combined them with hot colors: reds, pinks, oranges, and golds.

## ◈ Fabrics

Black solid (includes border strips and binding): 1⅜ yards

Multicolored wavy stripe: ⅛ yard

Red print: ⅛ yard

Orange print: ⅛ yard

Light yellow: ⅛ yard

Multicolored print: ⅛ yard

Reds, oranges, pinks, and golds: 1¼ yards **total**

Several black prints: 1 yard **total**

Border fabric: 1⅜ yards, OR, for a lengthwise border print stripe (with 5 repeats across): 3 yards

Backing: 2⅞ yards

Batting: 52″ × 52″

## ◈ Cutting fabrics

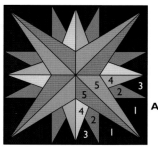

*Wishing Star block; 12″ block*

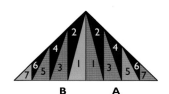

*Palm Leaf triangles*

*Note: All strips are cut from selvage to selvage and measure about 40″ long.*

| FABRIC | BLOCK | PATTERN AREA | CUT |
|---|---|---|---|
| Black solid | Wishing Star | A1, B1 | 1 strip 4¾″ |
| | | A3, B3 | 1 strip 2½″ |
| | | Border setting triangles | 1 square 7″; cut on both diagonals to make 4 triangles |
| | | Border strips | 10 strips 1½″ |
| | | Binding | 6 strips 2″ |
| Multicolored wavy stripe | Wishing Star | A5 | 1 strip 2½″ |
| Red print | Wishing Star | B5 | 1 strip 2½″ |
| Orange print | Wishing Star | A4 | 1 strip 2″ |
| Light yellow | Wishing Star | B4 | 1 strip 2″ |
| Multicolored print | Wishing Star | A2, B2 | 1 strip 2″ |
| Reds, oranges, pinks, and golds | Palm Leaf triangles | A: 1, 3, 5, 7<br>B: 1, 3, 5, 7 | 16 strips 2¼″ (total) |
| Black prints | Palm Leaf triangles | A: 2, 4, 6<br>B: 2, 4, 6 | 16 strips 2″ |

## Copying the patterns

Make 4 copies each of Wishing Star patterns A and B on page 65. Make 16 copies each of Palm Leaf patterns A and B on page 58. Cut out the patterns on the outer seamlines.

## Making the quilt

*See pages 29–39 for complete Quick-Strip Paper Piecing instructions.*

**1. Wishing Star block.** Make 4 A and 4 B Wishing Star units using the fabrics and strips indicated on the cutting chart. Sew the units into 4 pairs, pressing the seams open. Join the pairs into the block.

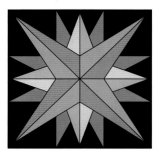

*Make 1 Wishing Star block.*

**2. Palm Leaf triangles.** Make 16 A and 16 B Palm Leaf units using the fabrics and strips indicated in the cutting chart. Sew the units into 16 triangle pairs as shown below. Press the seams open.

*Make 16 Palm Leaf triangles.*

**3. Center block unit.** Sew 4 of the Palm Leaf triangles to the Wishing Star block. Make a mark with a pin or fabric marking pencil ¼" in from each of the 4 corners.

**Mark ¼" in from each corner**

*Center block unit*

**4.** To add the first border, cut 4 strips 4" wide × at least 25" long from the border print fabric. (If you are using a border print fabric like I did, cut 4 identical strips.) Center the strips along the sides of the center block unit and pin them in place. If you are matching a border stripe, check to make sure the same print motif matches at the center and corners. Extra fabric will hang over beyond the edges. Sew the borders to the center block unit, stopping at the ¼" marks and backstitching.

**5.** To miter the corners, fold the block into a triangle and line up the border edges in one corner. With a right triangle ruler, or using the 45° angle on a straight ruler, draw the 45° angle from the point you backstitched out to the edge of the border corner.

*Drawing the 45° angle*

**6.** Pin along the drawn line, matching up the border print on both sides. Sew the seam and trim the seam allowance to ¼″. Press the seam to one side, or open if you prefer. Repeat for the other 3 corners.

**7.** To make the Palm Leaf border, cut 8 border strips 3″ wide × approximately 8″ long. (If you are using a border print fabric, cut identical strips.) Sew the strips to the short sides of the black setting triangles (cut as directed in the cutting chart), mitering the corner as shown in Steps 5 and 6. Match the print if using a border stripe. The strips and triangles are both oversized. Make 4.

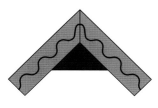

*Make 4.*

**8.** Sew a set of Palm Leaf triangles to either side of each of the black setting triangles, matching the mitered point with the Palm Leaf triangles. Trim the setting triangles even with the raw edges of the Palm Leaf triangles. The border strip should measure 6½″ wide after you trim. Sew the long side of each border to the quilt. See the Quilt Assembly Diagram on page 78.

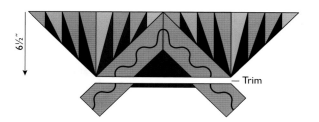

*Trim excess fabric. Make 4.*

**9.** For the border corners, cut 4 strips of border fabric 3″ wide × at least 18″ long. Sew a strip to each of the remaining 4 Palm Leaf triangles, centering the strip on the triangles. If you are using a border print fabric, cut identical strips and center them on the Palm Leaf triangles. Trim the excess border fabric even with the edges of the Palm Leaf triangles. Sew the border corners to the quilt. See the Quilt Assembly Diagram on page 78.

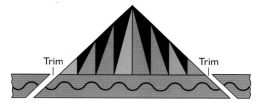

*Add border strips and trim. Make 4.*

**10.** To add outer borders, cut 4 border strips 4″ wide × at least 48″ long from the border print fabric, cutting identical pieces if you are matching stripes. Sew the 1½″-wide black fabric strips on either side of the border print strips, piecing strips together as needed to fit the border print strips. Pin and sew the borders to the quilt, matching the centers if you are using border stripes, and mitering the corners as shown in Steps 5 and 6 above.

**11.** I quilted the Wishing Star points with swirls and quilted curved lines in the Palm Leaf points, using red thread to contrast with the black background fabrics.

*Quilt Assembly Diagram*

# SNOW FLURRIES

*Snow Flurries,* by Peggy Martin, 2004. Quilt size: 40˝× 40˝.

As a child growing up in Ohio, I'd look forward with great anticipation to the first snowfall of winter. Catching snowflakes on my wool coat and looking in awe at their intricate lacy patterns for those few instants before the snowflakes melted was a favorite childhood activity. Making a snowflake quilt brings back those childhood memories—and these snowflakes won't melt! *Snow Flurries* is made up of paper-pieced snowflakes and appliquéd sun-printed snowflakes. Instructions for making sun-printed snowflakes follow the instructions for the paper-pieced blocks.

## Selecting fabrics

The simplest pieced snowflakes can be made using one white fabric for the snowflake and a background fabric. I found that using several different blue-and-white printed fabrics for the snowflake produces a lacier effect for more design interest. Setting the blocks with a printed snowflake fabric adds yet another design element.

## Fabrics and supplies

Dark blue for pieced block background: 1¼ yards

Flake fabrics: 1½ yards total **or** different blue-and-white prints as follows:

> Flake fabric 1: ½ yard
> Flake fabric 2 (includes inner border): ⅜ yard
> Flake fabric 3: ⅛ yard
> Flake fabric 4: ⅛ yard
> Flake fabric 5: ⅜ yard
> Flake fabric 6: ⅜ yard
> Flake fabric 7: ⅛ yard

Blue snowflake print (includes outer border and binding): 2 yards

Backing: 1⅜ yards

Batting: 45″ × 45″

15″ square quilting ruler (optional)

Lightweight cardboard or template plastic

**Supplies for sun-printed snowflakes:**

White fabric (PFD [prepared for dyeing] or other fabric that will absorb paint): 1 yard (See Resources, page 111, and note under Sun printing the snowflakes, page 84)

Invisible thread for appliqué

Setacolor transparent paints, blue and black (see Resources)

Freezer paper

Lightweight cardboard or template plastic

Rubber gloves

Foam brush

2 Styrofoam bowls or other containers (one for paint, one for water)

Spray bottle of water

20″ × 30″ foamcore board or other movable, rigid surface

Plastic trash bags, cut in half

Paper towels for cleanup

# ▓ Cutting fabrics

*Snowflake A; 12″ × 10⅜″ block*

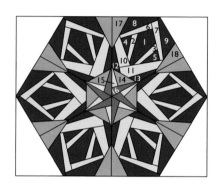

*Snowflake B; 12″ × 10⅜″ block*

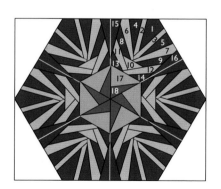

*Snowflake C; 12″ × 10⅜″ block*

| FABRIC | BLOCK | PATTERN AREA | CUT |
|---|---|---|---|
| Dark blue | A | 2, 3 | 2 strips 2″ |
| | A | 6, 7 | 2 strips 1¾″ |
| | A | 10, 11 | 2 strips 1¼″ |
| | B | 1 | 1 strip 2″ |
| | B | 4, 5 | 2 strips 1½″ |
| | B | 8, 9 | 2 strips 1¾″ |
| | B | 12, 13 | 2 strips 1¼″ |
| | C | 1 | 1 strip 2″ |
| | C | 4, 5, 15, 16 | 4 strips 1½″ |
| | C | 8, 9, 13, 14 | 4 strips 1¼″ |
| Flake fabric 1 | A | 1, 4, 5 | 3 strips 1½″ |
| | B | 2, 3 | 2 strips 1″ |
| | B | 6, 7, 15 | 3 strips 1¼″ |
| | B | 10, 11 | 2 strips 1½″ |
| Flake fabric 2 | A | 8, 9 | 2 strips 1¼″ |
| | | Inner border | 4 strips 1¾″ |
| Flake fabric 3 | A | 12 | 1 strip 1¼″ |
| | B | 16 | 1 strip 1¼″ |
| Flake fabric 4 | A | 13 | 1 strip 2½″ |
| Flake fabric 5 | B | 14 | 1 strip 1½″ |
| | B | 17, 18 | 2 strips 1¾″ |
| | C | 17 | 1 strip 2″ |
| Flake fabric 6 | C | 2, 3 | 2 strips 1″ |
| | C | 6, 7, 11, 12 | 4 strips 1¼″ |
| | C | 10 | 1 strip 1½″ |
| Flake fabric 7 | C | 18 | 1 strip 1½″ |
| Blue snowflake print | A, B, C | Setting triangles | 1 strip 4½″ |
| | | Side strips | 5 strips 3″ |
| | | Setting rectangles | 1 strip 14″ |
| | | Outer border | 4 strips 4″ |
| | | Binding | 5 strips 2″ |

*Note: All strips are cut from selvage to selvage and measure about 40″ long.*

*Some strips can be shared between blocks, so you may need fewer strips than are listed in the chart.*

## ▩ Copying the patterns

Make 6 copies **each** of Snowflake A, B, and C units on pages 88–90. Cut out the patterns on the outer dashed lines. Make 1 copy of the corner triangle pattern on page 87. Glue the corner triangle pattern to lightweight cardboard or template plastic. Cut out the pattern on the outer dashed lines.

## ▩ Making the pieced snowflakes

*See pages 29–39 for complete Quick-Strip Paper Piecing instructions.*

1. Cut 6 and 6 reversed corner triangles from the 4½″-wide strip of blue snowflake print. For ease of cutting, fold the strip in half. Place the template on top and cut out 6 times through the folded layers. This will automatically give you 6 triangles and 6 reversed triangles.

2. Make 6 units of Snowflake A using the fabrics and strips indicated in the cutting chart. Assemble the units into blocks by first sewing 2 pairs, then adding a third unit to make 2 halves of the block. Join the block halves to make the snowflake. Press all seams open. Sew 4 corner triangles to the 4 corners of the block as shown below. Press these seams toward the triangles to make a rectangular block.

*Make 2 halves of snowflake.*

*Join halves and add corner triangles.*

3. Make Snowflakes B and C following Step 2 above.

## ▩ Tilting the snowflakes

1. From the five 3″-wide strips of blue snowflake fabric, cut 6 rectangles 3″ × 12½″ and 6 rectangles 3″ × 15⅞″ (or lengths to fit your snowflakes). Sew the 12½″-long strips to 2 opposite sides of the snowflakes first, pressing the seams toward the strips, then add the 15⅞″-long strips to the other 2 sides, pressing the seams toward the strips.

2. Lay a square quilting ruler at an angle on top of each snowflake and trim the piece down to a 14″ square. The placement of the ruler can vary, depending on how you want the snowflake to tilt.

*Placing square-up ruler on block*

*Trimmed snowflake*

## ❄ Cutting setting pieces and assembling the quilt

**1.** Cut the following from the 14″-wide strip of blue snowflake fabric: 2 rectangles 4″ × 14″, 1 rectangle 8″ × 14″, and 1 rectangle 10″ × 14″. Cut another 2 rectangles 4″ × 14″, then piece them together end to end and trim to a rectangle 4″ × 17½″.

**2.** Assemble the quilt as shown in the Quilt Assembly Diagram. Sew the individual blocks and segments together first, then assemble in the order indicated by the numbered arrows, pressing the seams as you go.

**3.** Measure the quilt and cut the top and bottom inner border strips to fit. Sew the borders to the quilt. Press the seams toward the borders. Measure the quilt and add the side inner borders in the same manner. Repeat for the outer border.

*Quilt Assembly Diagram*

# Making sun-printed snowflakes

## CUTTING SNOWFLAKE DESIGNS

**1.** Copy 1 small, 1 medium, and 1 large hexagon pattern on page 87 for making snowflakes. Glue the 3 hexagon patterns to lightweight cardboard or template plastic and cut them out for use as master patterns.

**2.** Each snowflake will use 2 freezer-paper patterns: 1 for cutting the snowflake and 1 for basting it for appliqué. Trace the desired sizes of hexagons on freezer paper and cut out 2 identical hexagons for each snowflake you wish to make. Freezer paper can be folded in 4 layers and stapled together to speed up the cutting, making 4 hexagons at a time for each hexagon you draw. Select 2 hexagons the same size and set 1 aside to save for appliqué basting.

**3.** Fold the freezer paper hexagon as follows to cut the snowflake:

**First fold:** Fold the hexagon in half, bringing 2 straight sides together (1).

**Second and third folds:** Fold the left side triangles to the front (2); fold the right side triangles to the back (3) on the lines indicated below.

**Fourth fold:** Fold the triangle in half along the center (4). For less bulk, fold some layers to the front and other layers to the back.

*First fold*

*Second and third folds: fold side triangles.*

*Fourth fold*

**4.** Cut the snowflake as desired, experimenting with straight or curved lines. For the snowflake shapes, cut from one side to another side; for lacy holes, cut notches along the same side. Open out the folds to see the snowflake. Look at the sun-printed snowflakes on *Snow Flurries* for design ideas.

*Cutting a snowflake pattern*

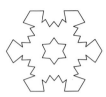

*Snowflake unfolded*

## SUN PRINTING THE SNOWFLAKES

Sun printing is an almost magical process. White fabric is painted with Setacolor transparent paint and opaque objects are placed on the wet paint. The fabric is then placed in the sun, and the fabric turns lighter underneath the objects as the paint dries, leaving an image of the object. This process works best on a sunny day with bright, direct sunlight. I find noontime to midafternoon in summer produces the best images, but a bright day in any season will produce fairly good images. I have also experimented with very bright lamps indoors, with mixed results (halogen lamps work best).

Note: PFD fabric is "prepared for dyeing" and has no finishes on it. (See Resources, page 111.) Any white fabric that will absorb paint easily will also work. Test white fabric by throwing a few sprinkles of water on the dry fabric. If water sinks in easily, the fabric should accept the paint. If water beads up on the fabric, it won't accept paint well. Try washing and drying it and testing it again. If water still beads up, use a different fabric.

**1.** Assemble the supplies listed on page 80. Have the cut freezer-paper snowflakes handy. Cover the foamcore board or other surface with a plastic trash bag piece. Cut the white fabric into fat quarters (approximately 18″ × 20″). Wearing rubber gloves, pour a little blue and black paint into a Styrofoam bowl and mix it to match your blue snowflake background. Add some water to the paint to make it the consistency of cream (usually about equal amounts of water and paint). The more water you add, the lighter the paint color will be. Add less water for a darker color.

**2.** Test a piece of fabric first. Lay a fat quarter of fabric on the plastic and pin it in place through the foamcore board. Use a spray bottle of water to slightly dampen the fabric. Paint a small section with the color you have mixed. Let it dry and compare it to the background fabric to see if you are satisfied with the color. If not, add varying amounts of blue, black, and water and test other areas on the fabric until you like the result.

**3.** To make the snowflakes, remove the test fabric and wipe off the plastic with a paper towel to clean the surface, or use a new piece of plastic if needed. Place a new fat quarter on the plastic and pin it to the board. Dampen it with the spray bottle of water, and paint the entire piece using the foam brush. While the paint is still wet, place the freezer-paper snowflakes **shiny side down** on the fabric, pressing them into the paint with your fingers and spacing them at least an inch apart to allow for seam allowances.

**4.** Place the board out in bright sunlight, preferably about midafternoon on a sunny day. Allow the paint to dry thoroughly. Gently lift off the freezer-paper patterns to reveal the sun-printed snowflakes. Print other fat quarters until you get the number of snowflakes needed. Iron the fabric on cotton setting, on both sides of the fabric, to set the paint. Save the freezer-paper snowflakes; they can be used again many times to sun print more fabric.

*Sun printing snowflakes*

## APPLIQUÉING THE SNOWFLAKES

**1.** Iron the extra freezer-paper hexagons (which you set aside earlier) on top of each snowflake of the same size. Cut out around each snowflake, adding at least a ¼″ seam allowance on all sides of the hexagon.

**2.** Remove the freezer-paper hexagons and flip the snowflake so the wrong side is up. Place the freezer-paper hexagon shiny side up on the snowflake and iron the raw edges back onto the freezer paper so they stick.

*Basting under raw edges onto freezer paper*

**3.** Try various arrangements of the basted snowflakes on the quilt until you are satisfied with their location. Iron them down, then place a few pins to make sure they don't move while you are sewing. Thread your machine with invisible thread, in both the top and the bobbin, and put a small needle (size 70 or 75) in your machine. If your machine won't accept invisible thread in the bobbin, use a blue cotton thread to match the background. Use a short narrow blind hem stitch or short narrow zigzag to appliqué the snowflakes to the background. (Refer to Step 11, page 101 for more details on blind hem stitch appliqué.) Begin near the corner of one side and work around each hexagon. Leave an opening of about 2″; reach under the hexagon and gently remove the freezer-paper hexagon. Continue stitching over the last 2″.

**4.** I quilted my snowflake quilt with silver metallic thread in free-motion swirling patterns to suggest the wind and the tumbling motion of the snowflakes falling.

***Night Blizzard,*** *by Peggy Martin, 2005. Quilt size: 41″ × 41″.*

This is the same pattern as *Snow Flurries*, but with black, gray, and silver fabrics for the background and snowflakes. A mottled charcoal-gray print was used instead of a snowflake print for the background.

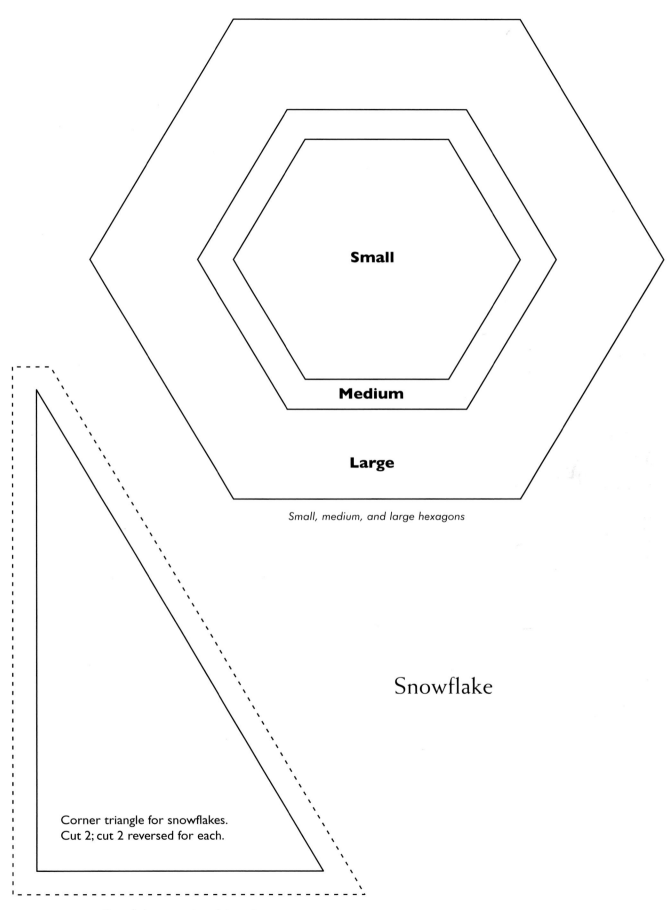

Small

Medium

Large

*Small, medium, and large hexagons*

Snowflake

Corner triangle for snowflakes.
Cut 2; cut 2 reversed for each.

*Snowflake corner template pattern*

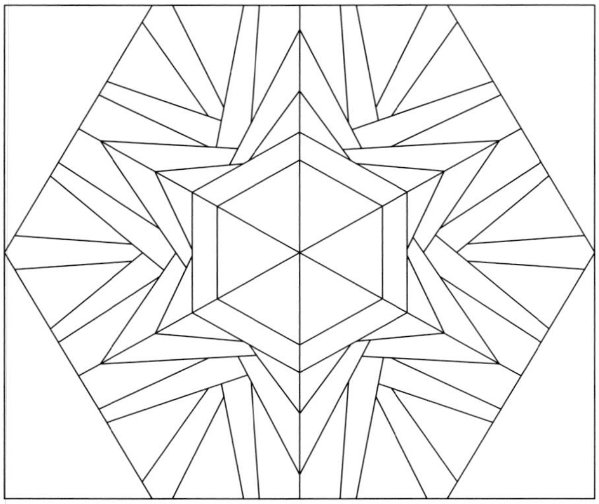

*Snowflake A; 12″ × 10⅜″ block*

# Snowflake (continued)

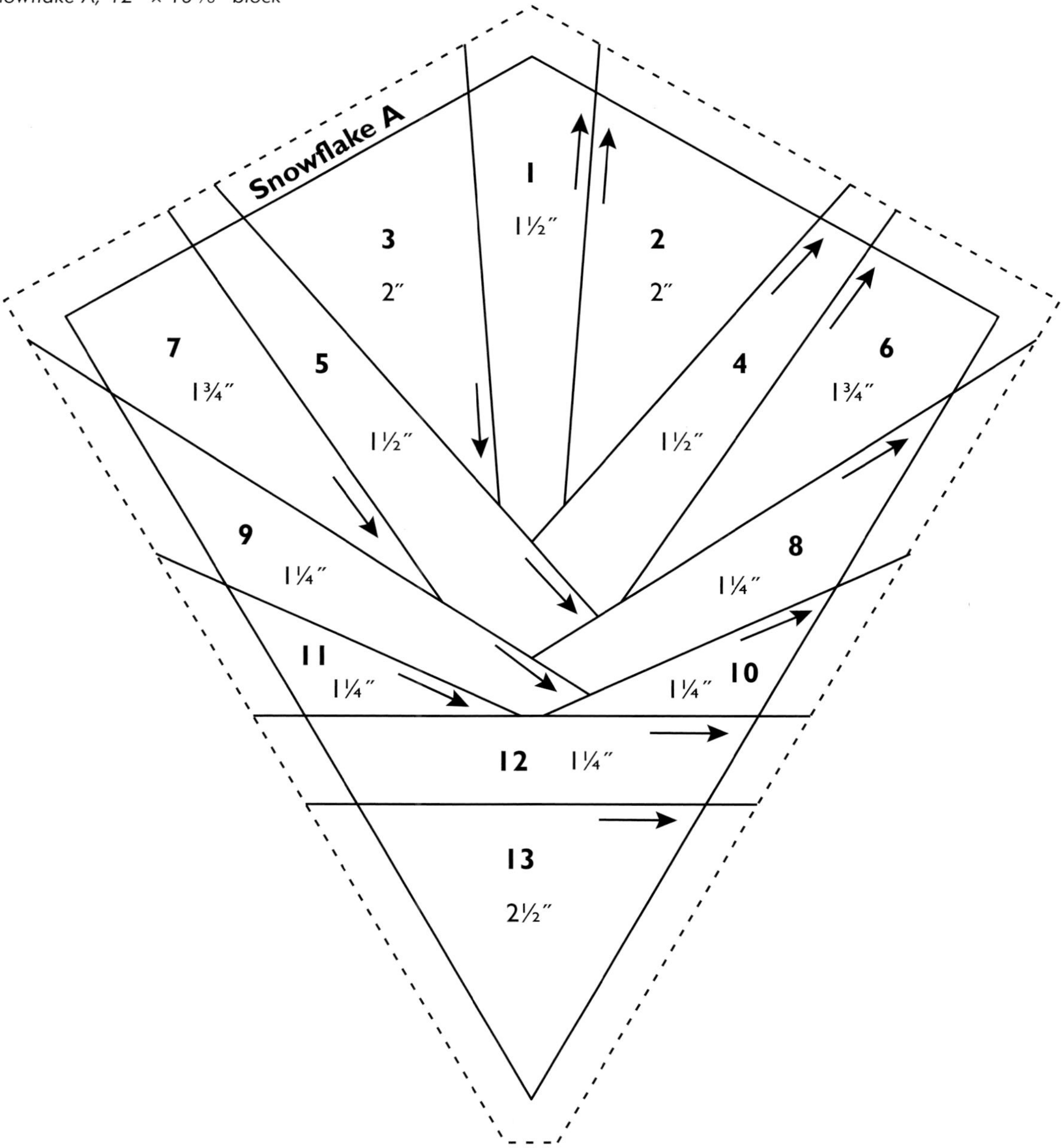

Snowflake A
1
1½″
2
2″
3
2″
4
1½″
5
1½″
6
1¾″
7
1¾″
8
1¼″
9
1¼″
10
1¼″
11
1¼″
12
1¼″
13
2½″


*Snowflake A unit*

*Note: See page 87 for corner template pattern.*

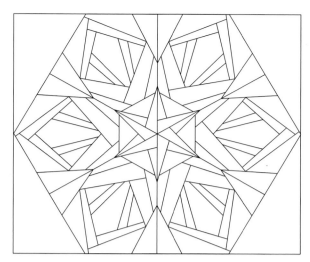

*Snowflake B; 12″ × 10⅜″ block*

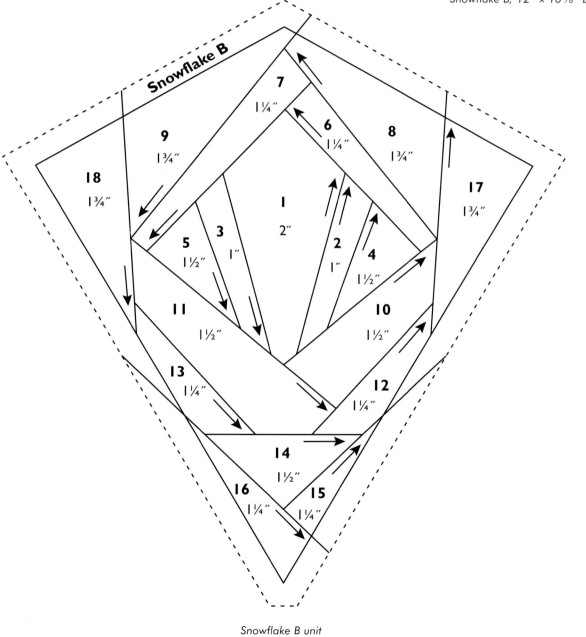

**Snowflake B**

7
1¼″

9
1¾″

6
1¼″

8
1¾″

18
1¾″

1
2″

17
1¾″

5
1½″

3
1″

2
1″

4
1½″

11
1½″

10
1½″

13
1¼″

12
1¼″

14
1½″

16
1¼″

15
1¼″

*Snowflake B unit*

*Note: See page 87 for corner template.*

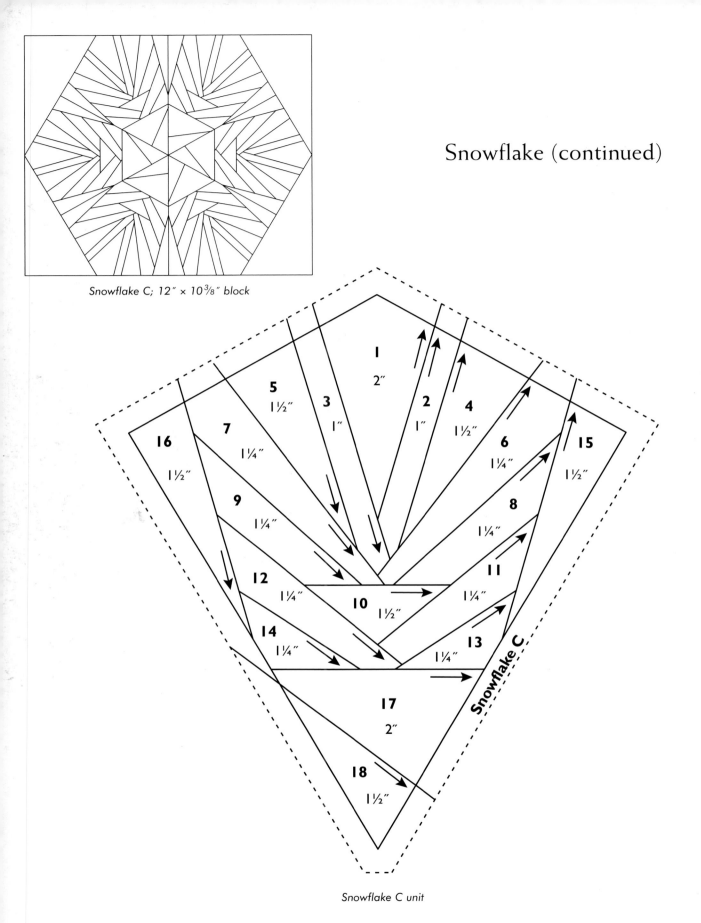

*Snowflake C; 12" × 10⅜" block*

# Snowflake (continued)

*Snowflake C unit*

*Note: See page 87 for corner template.*

# SNOWFLAKE PLACEMAT

*Snowflake placemat, by Peggy Martin, 2004. Quilt size: 18" × 12½".*

Snowflake placemats can be made very quickly using the sun-printing technique. Use one as a table centerpiece, or as a festive coffee-table mat for that plate of holiday cookies.

## Materials for each placemat

White fabric (prepared for dyeing or other fabric that will accept paint; see page 84 for details): 20″ × 14″

Blue fabric for binding: ⅛ yard

Batting: 21″ × 16″

Backing: 1 fat quarter

Sun-printing supplies (see page 80)

**1.** Make freezer-paper snowflakes following the instructions on page 84. You will need only 1 hexagon for each snowflake because these will not be appliquéd. Leftover freezer-paper snowflake patterns from the *Snow Flurries* project can also be used again to sun print placemats.

**2.** Paint the fabric on a protected surface as described on pages 84–85. Arrange the freezer-paper snowflakes on the wet paint as you desire, pressing them down into the paint with your finger so they stay in place. The placement will be the same on the finished placemat. Place the fabric in bright sunlight until it dries. Lift off the freezer paper and iron the fabric to set the paint.

**3.** Layer the sun-printed fabric with batting and backing and quilt with swirls, around the snowflakes, in a grid, or however you desire. Trim the quilt to 18″ × 12½″. Bind.

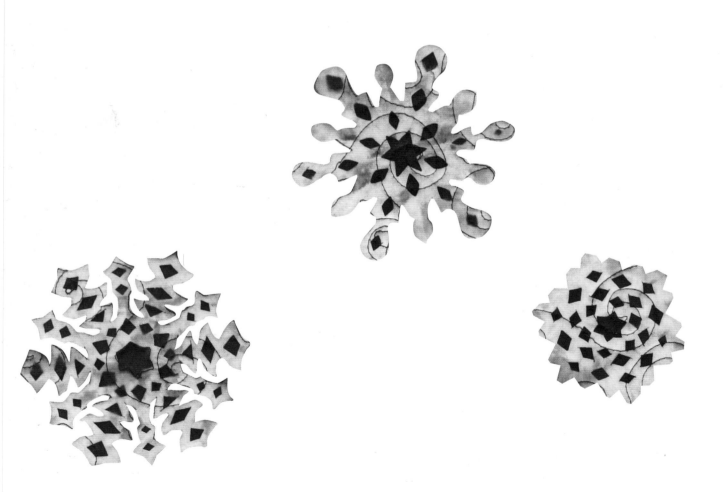

*Gypsy in My Soul,* by Peggy Martin, 2004. Quilt size: 50″ × 50″.

The idea of running away with the gypsies delighted me as a child. I love the bright colors and the feeling of motion that come across in this quilt. Working on these blocks was great fun and gave me a real feeling of freedom.

## Selecting fabrics

Black-and-white fabrics with a lot of movement were used for the backgrounds of brightly colored Evening Star blocks. The colorful print in the border is a fabric I had saved for just the right quilt.

## Fabrics

Assorted black-and-white prints: 1½ yards total or ¼ yard **each** of 9 fabrics

Assorted colors for star points: 2 yards total or ⅛ yard **each** of 45 fabrics

Black-with-brights print: 1 yard

Black-and-white dots: ½ yard

Border print: 1 yard

Black (includes binding): ½ yard

Backing: 3 yards

Batting: 55″ × 55″

Lightweight cardboard, template plastic, or freezer paper

## Cutting fabrics

*Evening Star, 12″ block*

| FABRIC | PATTERN AREA | CUT |
|---|---|---|
| 9 assorted black-and-white prints | 2, 3 | 2 strips 2¾″ of **each** fabric |
| 9 assorted colors | 1 | 1 strip 1¾″ of **each** fabric |
| | 4 | 1 strip 1½″ of **each** fabric |
| | 5 | 1 strip 1½″ of **each** fabric |
| | 6 | 1 strip 1¼″ of **each** fabric |
| | 7 | 1 strip 1½″ of **each** fabric |
| Black-with-brights print | Setting piece | 5 strips 6½″ |
| Black-and-white dots | Sashing | 4 strips 2½″ |
| Black | Sashing squares | 1 strip 2½″; cut into 4 squares 2½″ × 2½″ |
| | Binding | 6 strips 2″ |
| Large print | Border | 5 strips 5½″ |

*Note: All strips are cut from selvage to selvage and measure about 40″ long.*

# Copying the patterns

Make 72 copies of the Evening Star pattern on page 96. Cut out these patterns on the outer seamlines. For the setting template, make 1 copy of the 12″ Block Circle Setting Template on page 28, but do not cut it out yet; it will be used later to make a template.

# Making the quilt

*See pages 29–39 for complete Quick-Strip Paper Piecing instructions.*

1. Make 9 Evening Star blocks, each one composed of 8 block units, using the fabrics indicated in the cutting chart. For scrappy blocks like the ones I made, use 2 strips of the same black-and-white background fabric for areas 2 and 3; use 1 strip of assorted fabrics for each of the other areas of one 8-unit block. If you are making all your blocks the same, you may save a strip or 2 by sharing strips between blocks. Remove the paper after the units are pieced or before sewing them into a circle, or leave it in until later, as you choose.

2. Sew the 8 units of each block into pairs, pressing the seams open. Join the pairs into 2 groups of 4 units to make the 2 halves of the block, again pressing the seams open. Join the 2 halves to make the circle. Make 9 circles.

*Sewing units into a circle*

3. Glue the copy of the 12″ Block Circle Setting Template on page 28 to a piece of light cardboard or template plastic. Or, if you prefer, trace the template onto freezer paper. Fold the 6½″ strips of black-with-brights fabric into fourths. Place the template on top and trace it, or iron freezer paper to the fabric to use as a template. Cut through the 4 layers, making 4 corner setting pieces at once. Turn the template and cut another set of 4 from the same strip. Transfer the match points to the seam

allowances where indicated. Make 9 sets of 4 setting pieces for the 9 blocks.

4. Sew 4 setting pieces together on the short seams to form a square with a circle hole in the center. Press the seams open. Make 9.

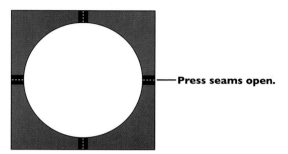

*Make 9 setting squares.*

5. Pin the setting squares to the Evening Star circles with the setting squares on top, matching the seams of the circle to the match points and the seams on the setting squares. Sew the curved seam and press toward the setting pieces.

*Sew setting pieces to circle.*

6. Cut 12 sashing pieces 2½″ × 12½″ (or size to fit your blocks). Lay out the blocks, sashing strips, and sashing squares following the Quilt Assembly Diagram. Sew the blocks and sashing together in rows, pressing toward the sashing. Sew the rows together to make the body of the quilt.

7. Measure the quilt and cut the top and bottom border strips to fit. Sew the borders to the quilt. Press the seams toward the borders. Add the side borders in the same manner.

8. I quilted my star points with wavy lines, and then I quilted swirls and loop patterns in the backgrounds and border.

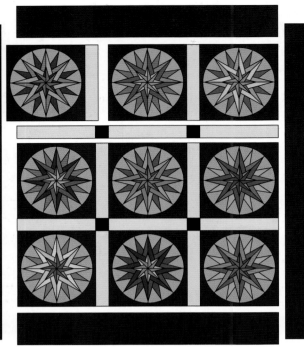

*Quilt Assembly Diagram*

*Evening Star; 12″ block (11″ circle)*

# Evening Star

*Note: For circle setting template pattern, see page 28.*

**3**

2¾″

**2**

2¾″

**1**

1¾″

**4**

1½″

**5**

1½″

**6**

1¼″

**7**

1½″

# SUMMER IN PROVENCE

*Summer in Provence,* by Peggy Martin, 2004. Quilt size: 36" × 36".

Circle designs are a favorite of mine. I added two more circular rings to the Evening Star block to expand the center circle. The curved pieced borders continue the curved design element. The juxtaposition of all the long, sharp points with the curved elements creates a dynamic design.

##  Selecting fabrics

Yellows and blues make a crisp, classic color scheme. The enlarged circle in yellows and blues is like radiant summer sunshine, and the blue-and-yellow floral is reminiscent of fabrics from Provence. I used several different blues and yellows throughout the quilt for a scrap look.

## Fabrics

Dark blue(s)
(includes binding): 1¾ yards

Bright yellow(s): 1⅝ yards

Light yellow: ⅛ yard

Light blue: ¼ yard

Blue print: ¼ yard

Blue/yellow stripe: ⅜ yard

Blue-and-yellow
large floral: 1½ yards

Backing: 1¼ yards

Batting: 41″ × 41″

Invisible thread

Freezer paper

Fabric gluestick

Lightweight cardboard or
template plastic (optional)

## Cutting fabrics

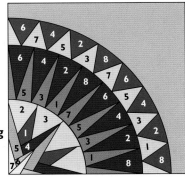

*Summer in Provence, ¼ of 24″ block*

*Curved border*

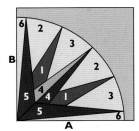

*Border corner*

| FABRIC | BLOCK | PATTERN AREA | CUT |
|---|---|---|---|
| Dark blue(s) | Evening Star | 4 | 1 strip 1½″ |
| | Ring 1 | 2, 4, 6, etc. (even #s) | 4 strips 2½″ |
| | Ring 2 | 2, 4, 6, etc. (even #s) | 3 strips 2¾″ |
| | Border | 2, 4, 6, etc. (even #s) | 15 strips 1¾″ |
| | Border corners | A4 | 1 strip 1¼″ |
| | | A5, B5 | 2 strips 1¾″ |
| | Binding | | 4 strips 2″ |
| Bright yellow(s) | Evening Star | 2, 3 | 2 strips 2¾″ |
| | Evening Star | 6 | 1 strip 1¼″ |
| | Ring 2 | 1, 3, 5, etc. (odd #s) | 3 strips 2½″ |
| | Border | 1, 3, 5, etc. (odd #s) | 15 strips 1¾″ |
| | Border corners | A2, A3, B2, B3 | 3 strips 2½″ |
| | | A6, B6 | 2 strips 1¼″ |
| Light yellow | Evening Star | 7 | 1 strip 1½″ |
| Light blue | Evening Star | 5 | 2 strips 1½″ |
| | Border corners | B4 | 1 strip 1¼″ |
| Blue print | Evening Star | 1 | 1 strip 1¾″ |
| | Border corners | A1, B1 | 2 strips 1¾″ |
| Blue/yellow stripe | Ring 1 | 1, 3, 5, etc. (odd #s) | 4 strips 1¾″ |
| Blue/yellow floral | Center circle | Setting template | 1 strip 12½″ |
| | Curved border | Setting template | 1 strip 18″ |
| | Border corners | Setting template | 1 strip 6½″ |

## Copying the patterns

Make 8 copies each of the following: Evening Star pattern on page 96, Ring 1 and Ring 2 patterns on pages 104–105, and Border A and Border B patterns on pages 107–108. Make 4 copies each of Border Corner A and Border Corner B patterns on page 109. Cut out these patterns on the outside dashed lines.

For setting templates, make 1 copy of the 12″ Block Circle Setting pattern on page 28 and 1 copy of the Curved Border Setting pattern on page 110. Make 1 copy each of the 24″ Block Circle Setting pattern, parts A and B, on page 106. Do not cut these out yet; they will be used later to make freezer-paper templates.

## Making the quilt

*See pages 29–39 for complete Quick-Strip Paper Piecing instructions.*

**1. Center block.** Make 8 Evening Star units using the fabrics and strips indicated in the cutting chart. The paper can be removed now or left in until later, as you choose. Sew the units into pairs, pressing the seams open. Join the pairs into 2 groups of 4 units to make the 2 halves of the block, again pressing the seams open. Join the 2 halves of the block to make the Evening Star center block.

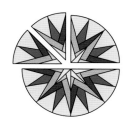

*Evening Star construction*

**2. Ring 1.** Make the 8 units of Ring 1 all at the same time using the fabrics and strips indicated in the cutting chart. Sew the units together to make a continuous ring. Press the seams open. Trim the curved edges exactly to the outer dashed line. Transfer the match-point marks to the fabric in the seam allowance using a fabric marking pencil. Carefully remove the paper from the ring.

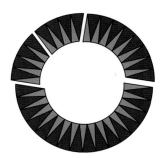

*Ring 1 construction*

**3. Ring 2.** Make the 8 units for Ring 2 all at the same time using the fabrics and strips indicated in the cutting chart. Sew the units together to make a continuous ring. Press the seams open. Trim the curved edges exactly to the outer dashed line. Transfer the match-point marks to the fabric in the seam allowance. Carefully remove the paper from the ring.

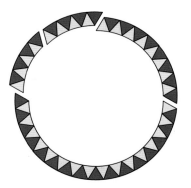

*Ring 2 construction*

**4.** Sew Ring 1 to the center Evening Star circle, pinning and matching the seams in the Evening Star to the match points indicated on Ring 1. Press the seams in either direction, as you choose. Sew Ring 2 to Ring 1, pinning and matching the seams where indicated. Press the seams in either direction.

**5. Adding setting corners.** Tape parts A and B of the 24″ Block Circle Setting pattern together where indicated to make a complete template pattern. Fold a large piece of freezer paper in half and place the corner of the complete Circle Setting pattern on the fold where indicated. Staple the pattern in place, taking care not to distort the pattern or the freezer paper. Cut the template out of the freezer paper and remove the staples. Transfer the marks for matching points, adding a match point at the folds.

**6.** Fold the 12½˝ strip of blue and yellow large floral fabric in half. Iron the Circle Setting template to the strip with one straight edge along the cut edge of the fabric. Cut 2 Circle Setting pieces. Rotate the template 180° so a straight edge is along the top cut edge of the fabric. Iron the template in place and cut the remaining 2 setting pieces. Transfer the match points to the seam allowances where indicated.

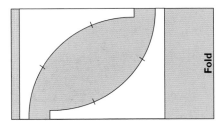

**7.** Sew the 4 short seams to make the setting square. Pin and match the seams and matching points to the points on Ring 2, with the setting square on top. Sew the seam. Press the seam allowance toward the setting corners.

*Add setting corners*

## Sewing the borders

**1.** Each side of the border is made up of 2 A border sections and 2 B border sections. You will piece the 4 borders at one time. Beginning with 4 Border A patterns, piece the areas from 1 to 10, using the strips indicated in the cutting chart. Take care not to short areas when cutting units apart.

**2.** After piecing area 10, line up the first line on the Border B pattern with the inner seamline at the end of Border A. Tape Border B in place so the 2 lines match up. Add a Border B pattern to the other 3 borders in the same way.

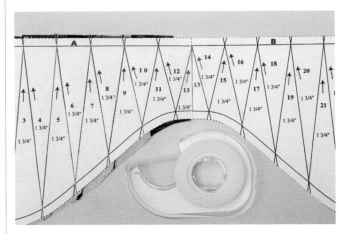

*Adding the next border section*

**3.** Continue piecing the 4 borders. When you get to area 13, where A and B join, do not sew on the vertical joining line; 1 piece of background fabric will cover the entire area.

**4.** Continue piecing the 4 borders along strips until you get close to the end of the Border B section. Add on another Border A to each of the 4 borders, trimming off the seam allowance on the new piece and taping it to the end of the border, matching lines as before. (The numbers will begin with 1 again, but continue piecing in order down the units, again ignoring the vertical joining seam and treating area 25 and area 1 as one area.) Continue piecing, and add on the last Border B section as before, then piece to the end of Border B. Trim any excess fabric away from the edges of the patterns.

**5. Making the setting pieces.** Place a copy of the Curved Border Setting Template pattern on a piece of folded freezer paper, matching the fold lines. Staple it in place. Cut it out on the outer lines. Remove the staples with a staple remover and open out the template. Iron the template to a piece of lightweight cardboard or template plastic, making a master pattern. Use the master pattern to make 8 freezer-paper patterns, cutting them out on the outer lines (or the freezer paper can be folded into layers and stapled to cut multiple patterns at once, if you like).

**6.** Fold the large floral print in half. Arrange 4 of the freezer-paper patterns on the fabric to make best use of the fabric, making sure to allow room for the added ¼″ seam allowance on the curved edge and keeping the straight edges of the patterns on the straight grain of the fabric. Iron the patterns in place. When cutting out the patterns, **add a generous ¼″ seam allowance on the curved edge** of each pattern. (Because the fabric is folded double, you will get 8 setting pieces from the 4 patterns.)

**7.** Remove the freezer paper from the fabric. Join the fabric setting pieces into pairs by seaming them together on the short side seam allowance. You will have 4 pairs for the 4 sides of the quilt.

**8. Basting the setting pieces for appliqué.** Flip over the fabric setting pairs to the wrong side. On the 8 freezer-paper patterns, fold under ¼″ on the short sides (where the seams were sewn). Using a gluestick, place a few spots of glue on the dull side of the freezer paper in the 2 corners and along the top edge of the curve. Position the freezer paper shiny side up on the wrong side of the fabric pairs, lining up the straight edge along the bottom. The curved edge will have fabric showing for the seam allowance. Clip the concave (valley) edges of the curves almost down to the freezer paper.

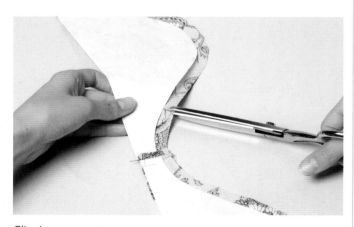

*Clipping concave curves*

**9.** Using a dry iron, pull the fabric over the freezer-paper edge and press it to the freezer paper. The shiny side of the freezer paper will hold the fabric in place.

*Basting under the curved edges*

**10. Basting the setting pieces to the border.** Apply glue to the basted seam allowances on the setting pieces and baste them to the curved edge of the paper-pieced border.

*Basting setting pieces to border*

**11. Machine appliqué.** Set your machine to the blind hem stitch with a very narrow width (.5 to 1) and a very small stitch length (.5 to 1). Using invisible thread in the top and bobbin, appliqué the curved edge. The straight stitches will ride along the tips of the points, next to the fold, with the zigzag stitch coming up onto the edge of the floral setting fabric. Remove the freezer paper before assembling the quilt.

*Blind hem stitch*

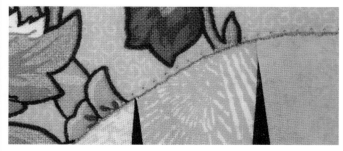

*Blind hem stitch*

**12. Piece the border corners.** Piece 4 of Border Corner A using the strips indicated in the cutting chart. Piece 4 of Border Corner B. Sew units A and B together to make the quarter-circle. Press the seams open. Make a freezer-paper template from the copy of the circle setting pattern for the 12″ block. Iron the freezer-paper pattern to the 6½″ strip of large floral fabric. Cut out 4 setting pieces and sew them to the pieced border corners, matching the center seam to the match point on the setting piece.

*Make 4 border corners.*

**13. Assemble the quilt** following the Quilt Assembly Diagram.

**14.** I quilted my quilt with curving lines in the points and swirls in the setting pieces.

*Quilt Assembly Diagram*

*Good Vibrations, by Peggy Martin, 2005. Quilt size: 48″ × 48″.*

I tie-dyed some beautiful colors in a circular design and wanted to use them in a special quilt. I also wanted to place the Evening Star with added rings on point. It seemed natural to fill in the corner setting triangles with the tie-dyed fabric, producing a radiating effect. The same curved border pattern was used, extended with an extra section to make it fit the larger square.

Shelley Gragg used the Evening Star with added rings as the center of a bed-sized medallion quilt, placing the square on point. The center is bordered with Evening Star blocks, also placed on point.

*Anne's Quilt,* by Shelley Gragg, 2002. Quilt size: 96″ × 84″.
Machine quilted by Carolyn Reynolds. Collection of Steve and Anne Ford.
Photo by Sharon Risedorph.

The Evening Star with Ring 1 added radiates into space with soft-edge appliqué rays. The wavy striped fabric enhances the outward motion.

*Solar Wind,* by Peggy Martin, 2005. Quilt size: 36″ × 24″.

# Summer in Provence

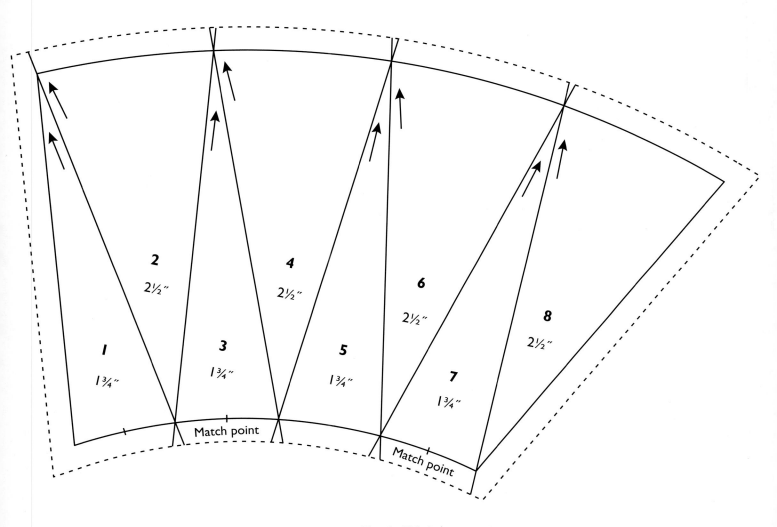

**2**

2½"

**4**

2½"

**6**

2½"

**8**

2½"

**1**

1¾"

**3**

1¾"

**5**

1¾"

**7**

1¾"

Match point

Match point

*Ring 1; 19" circle*

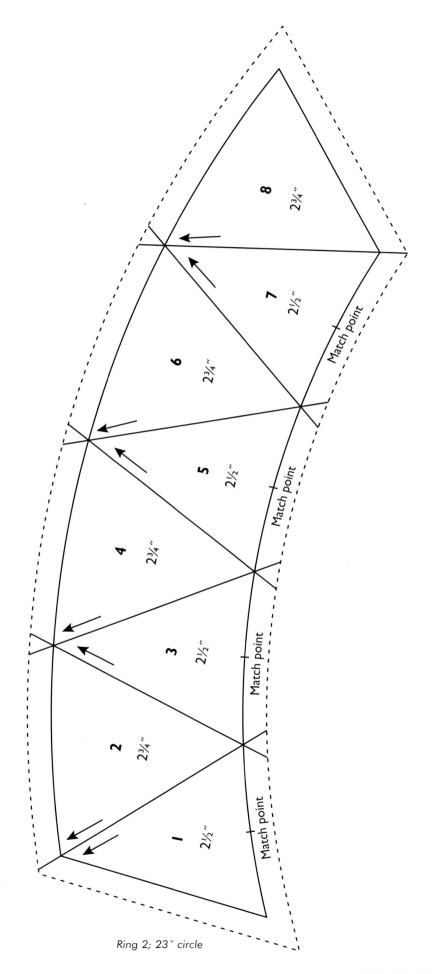

*Ring 2; 23″ circle*

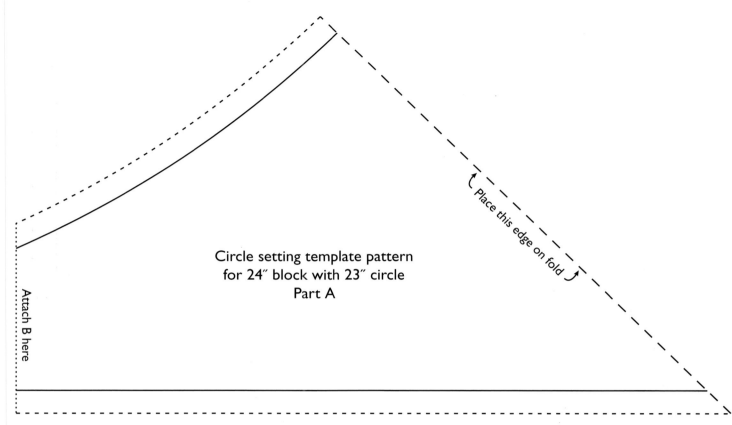

Circle setting template pattern
for 24″ block with 23″ circle
Part A

Attach B here

Place this edge on fold

*Circle setting pattern A*

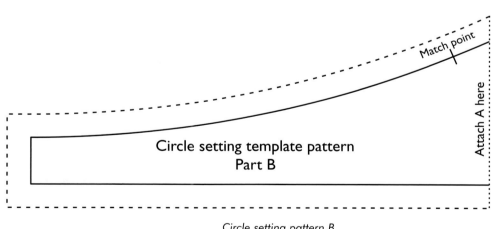

Match point

Circle setting template pattern
Part B

Attach A here

*Circle setting pattern B*

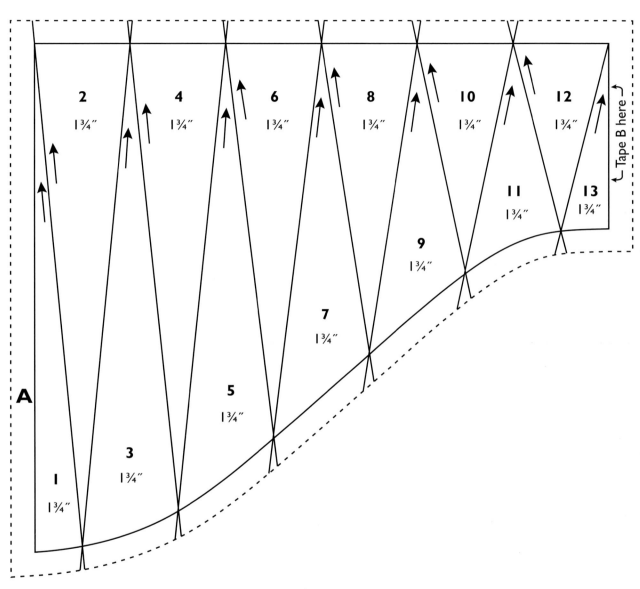

**A**

**2**
1¾"

**4**
1¾"

**6**
1¾"

**8**
1¾"

**10**
1¾"

**12**
1¾"

**11**
1¾"

**13**
1¾"

**9**
1¾"

**7**
1¾"

**5**
1¾"

**3**
1¾"

**1**
1¾"

↰ Tape B here ↲

*Border A*

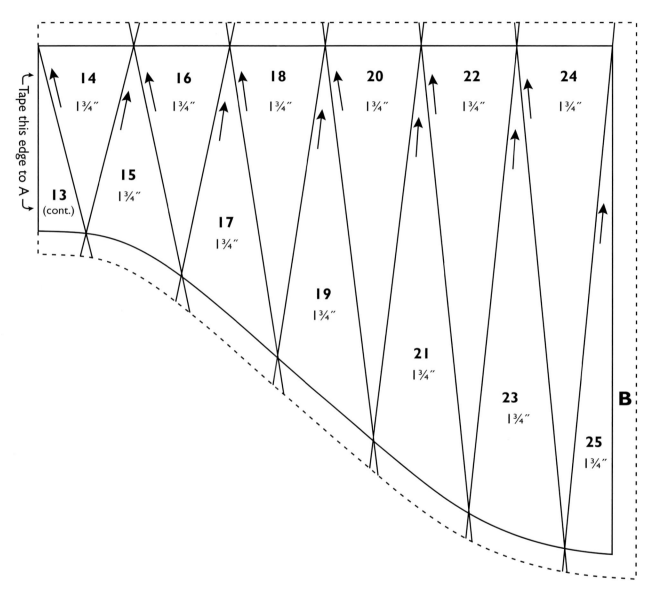

Border B

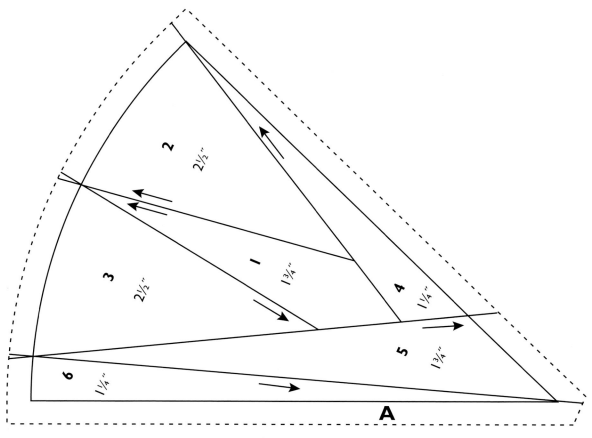

Border Corner A

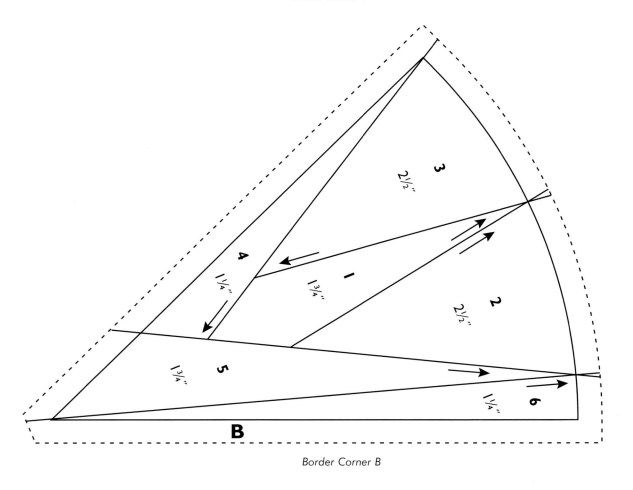

Border Corner B

# Summer in Provence (continued)

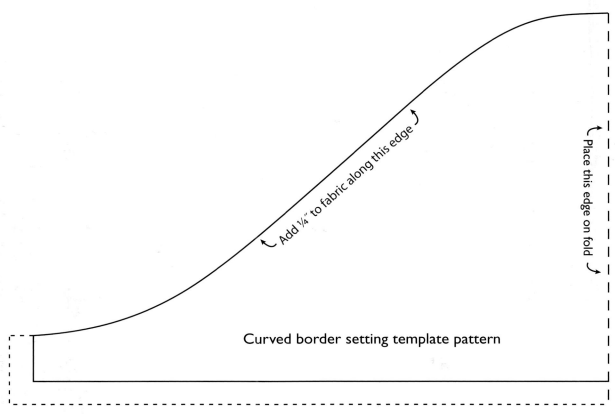

Add ¼" to fabric along this edge

Place this edge on fold

**Curved border setting template pattern**

*Curved border setting template pattern*

# ABOUT THE AUTHOR

Peggy Martin has been fascinated by the quilting world since she began quilting in 1981. A quilting teacher since 1985, she became interested in developing and teaching quicker techniques that produce great designs in a fraction of the time. Her first book, *Quick-Strip Paper Piecing*, applied a strip-pieced assembly-line approach to paper piecing, revolutionizing and greatly speeding up the process.

Working with color and experimenting with new color combinations and unusual fabrics are some of her trademarks. Her exploration of different design possibilities continues to guide her in discovering new ways to expand on tradition. Her enthusiastic students are inspired to explore their own expressions in both color and design.

Peggy was born in Ohio and has lived in Southern California since 1970. She has a degree in music and plays piano, guitar, and harp when she isn't quilting, teaching, or traveling. She lives in San Diego and is married with two grown sons.

# RESOURCES

For Setacolor paints and prepared-for-dyeing fabric, plus free catalogs:

DHARMA TRADING COMPANY
Box 150916
San Rafael, CA 94915
1-800-542-5227
www.dharmatrading.com

PRO CHEMICAL & DYE, INC.
Box 14
Somerset MA 02726
1-800-228-9393
www.prochemical.com

For foundation papers:

C&T PUBLISHING, INC.
1-800-284-1114
www.ctpub.com

For quilting supplies:

COTTON PATCH MAIL ORDER
3404 Hall Lane
Dept. CTB
Lafayette, CA 94549
800-835-4418 or
925-283-7883
www.quiltusa.com

# Great Titles from C&T PUBLISHING

**Carol Doak's** Simply *Sensational* 9-Patch Stars

BONUS Foundation Factory CD Included

· 12 QUILT PROJECTS · MIX & MATCH UNITS TO CREATE A GALAXY OF PAPER-PIECED STARS

**Paper Piecing** *with* Alex Anderson

■ Tips
■ Techniques
■ 6 Projects

Host of Simply Quilts HGTV

**THE EXPERTS' GUIDE TO FOUNDATION PIECING**
**15 TECHNIQUES & PROJECTS**

Barbara Barber
Carol Doak
Cynthia England
Caryl Bryer Fallert
Lynn Graves
Lesly-Claire Greenberg
Dixie Haywood
Peggy Martin
Judy Mathieson
Ruth B. McDowell
Anita Grossman Solomon
Eileen Sullivan
Barb Vlack

**JANE HALL**

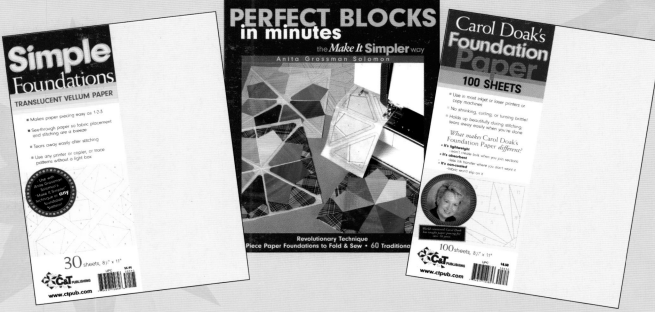

# Simple Foundations
### TRANSLUCENT VELLUM PAPER

■ Makes paper piecing easy as 1-2-3

■ See-through paper so fabric placement and stitching are a breeze

■ Tears away easily after stitching

■ Use any printer or copier, or trace patterns without a light box

Use with Anita Grossman Solomon's "Make It Simpler" technique or any foundation pattern

30 sheets, 8½" x 11"

www.ctpub.com

**PERFECT BLOCKS in minutes**
the *Make It Simpler* way
Anita Grossman Solomon

Revolutionary Technique
Piece Paper Foundations to Fold & Sew · 60 Traditional

# Carol Doak's Foundation Paper
### 100 SHEETS

■ Use in most inkjet or laser printers or copy machines

■ No shrinking, curling, or turning brittle!

■ Holds up beautifully during stitching; tears away easily when you're done

*What makes Carol Doak's Foundation Paper different:*
■ **It's lightweight**
—won't create bulk when you join sections
■ **It's absorbent**
—less ink transfer where you don't want it
■ **It's non-coated**
—fabric won't slip on it

World-renowned Carol Doak has taught paper piecing for over 10 years

100 sheets, 8½" x 11"

www.ctpub.com